CYBERSECURITY, CYBERANALYSIS AND WARNING

CYBERSECURITY, CYBERANALYSIS AND WARNING

KERRY T. NORWOOD
AND SANDRA P. CATWELL
EDITORS

Nova Science Publishers, Inc.
New York

Copyright © 2009 by Nova Science Publishers, Inc.

All rights reserved. No part of this book may be reproduced, stored in a retrieval system or transmitted in any form or by any means: electronic, electrostatic, magnetic, tape, mechanical photocopying, recording or otherwise without the written permission of the Publisher.

For permission to use material from this book please contact us:
Telephone 631-231-7269; Fax 631-231-8175
Web Site: http://www.novapublishers.com

NOTICE TO THE READER
The Publisher has taken reasonable care in the preparation of this book, but makes no expressed or implied warranty of any kind and assumes no responsibility for any errors or omissions. No liability is assumed for incidental or consequential damages in connection with or arising out of information contained in this book. The Publisher shall not be liable for any special, consequential, or exemplary damages resulting, in whole or in part, from the readers' use of, or reliance upon, this material.

Independent verification should be sought for any data, advice or recommendations contained in this book. In addition, no responsibility is assumed by the publisher for any injury and/or damage to persons or property arising from any methods, products, instructions, ideas or otherwise contained in this publication.

This publication is designed to provide accurate and authoritative information with regard to the subject matter covered herein. It is sold with the clear understanding that the Publisher is not engaged in rendering legal or any other professional services. If legal or any other expert assistance is required, the services of a competent person should be sought. FROM A DECLARATION OF PARTICIPANTS JOINTLY ADOPTED BY A COMMITTEE OF THE AMERICAN BAR ASSOCIATION AND A COMMITTEE OF PUBLISHERS.

LIBRARY OF CONGRESS CATALOGING-IN-PUBLICATION DATA

Available upin request.

ISBN: 978-1-60692-658-1

Published by Nova Science Publishers, Inc. ✦ New York

CONTENTS

Preface		**vii**
Chapter 1	Cyber Analysis and Warning. DHS Faces Challenges in Establishing a Comprehensive National Capability *U.S Government Accountability Office*	**1**
Chapter 2	Critical Infrastructure Protection. DHS Needs to Better Address Its Cybersecurity Responsibilities *David Powner*	**61**
Chapter 3	Critical Infrastructure Protection. DHS Needs to Fully Address Lessons Learned from Its First Cyber Storm Exercise *U.S Government Accountability Office*	**75**
Index		**109**

PREFACE

Cyber analysis and warning capabilities are critical to thwarting computer-based (cyber) threats and attacks. The Department of Homeland Security (DHS) established the United States Computer Emergency Readiness Team (US-CERT) to, among other things, coordinate the nation's efforts to prepare for, prevent, and respond to cyber threats to systems and communications networks. The authors' objectives were to (1) identify key attributes of cyber analysis and warning capabilities, (2) compare these attributes with US-CERT's current capabilities to identify whether there are gaps, and (3) identify US-CERT's challenges to developing and implementing key attributes and a successful national cyber analysis and warning capability. To address these objectives, the authors identified and analyzed related documents, observed operations at numerous entities, and interviewed responsible officials and experts.

In: Cybersecurity, Cyberanalysis and Warning ISBN: 978-1-60692-658-1
Editors: K. T. Norwood et al © 2009 Nova Science Publishers, Inc.

Chapter 1

CYBER ANALYSIS AND WARNING. DHS FACES CHALLENGES IN ESTABLISHING A COMPREHENSIVE NATIONAL CAPABILITY[*]

U.S Government Accountability Office

ABBREVIATIONS

CERT/CC	CERT Coordination Center
DHS	Department of Homeland Security
DOD	Department of Defense
HITRAC	Homeland Infrastructure Threat and Risk Analysis Center
HSPD	Homeland Security Presidential Directive
ISAC	information sharing and analysis center
NCRCG	National Cyber Response Coordination Group
NCSD	National Cyber Security Division
NIST	National Institute of Standards and Technology
OMB	Office of Management and Budget
US-CERT	United States Computer Emergency Readiness Team

---

[*] Excerpted from GAO Report GAO-08-588, dated July 2008.

July 31, 2008

The Honorable
James R. Langevin
Chairman

The Honorable
Michael T. McCaul
Ranking Member

Subcommittee on Emerging Threats,
Cybersecurity, and Science and Technology
Committee on Homeland SecurityHouse of Representatives

The rapid increase in computer connectivity has revolutionized the way that our government, our nation, and much of the world communicate and conduct business. While the benefits have been enormous, this widespread interconnectivity also poses significant risks to our nation's computer-reliant critical operations. Establishing analytical and warning capabilities is essential to thwarting computer-based, or cyber, threats and attacks. Cyber analysis and warning capabilities include (1) monitoring network activity to detect anomalies, (2) analyzing information and investigating anomalies to determine whether they are threats, (3) warning appropriate officials with timely and actionable threat and mitigation information, and (4) responding to the threat.

Federal law and policy direct the Department of Homeland Security (DHS) to establish such capabilities for our nation. To fulfill this requirement, the department established the United States Computer Emergency Readiness Team (US-CERT) to develop and implement these capabilities and, in doing so, coordinate the nation's efforts to prepare for, prevent, and respond to cyber threats and attacks.

Our objectives were to (1) identify key attributes of cyber analysis and warning capabilities, (2) compare these attributes with US-CERT's current analysis and warning capabilities to identify whether there are gaps, and (3) identify US-CERT's challenges to developing and implementing key attributes and a successful national cyber analysis and warning capability. To identify key attributes, we identified and analyzed relevant laws, strategies, policies, reports, and studies; observed cyber analysis and warning operations at numerous entities; and interviewed responsible officials and experts from federal and nonfederal entities.[1] To determine US-CERT's current capabilities and related challenges, we analyzed DHS's policies, procedures, and program plans and interviewed relevant officials. Appendix I provides further details on our objectives, scope, and methodology.

We conducted this performance audit from June 2007 to July 2008 in accordance with generally accepted government auditing standards. Those standards require that we plan and perform the audit to obtain sufficient, appropriate evidence to provide a reasonable basis for our findings and conclusions based on our audit objectives. We believe that the evidence obtained provides a reasonable basis for our findings and conclusions based on our audit objectives.

RESULTS IN BRIEF

Cyber analysis and warning typically encompasses four key capabilities: monitoring, analysis, warning, and response. Monitoring system and communication networks includes activities to detect cyber threats, attacks, and vulnerabilities. Analysis involves taking the information gathered from monitoring and hypothesizing about what the threat or attack might be, investigating it, and identifying any impact and, if necessary, mitigation steps. Warning includes alerting recipients about potential or imminent, as well as ongoing, cyber threats or attacks. Response includes containing and recovering from cyber incidents that occur. Our research and past experience identified 15 key attributes associated with these cyber analysis and warning capabilities, as shown in the following table:

Table 1. Attributes of Cyber Analysis and Warning

Capability	Attribute
Monitoring	Establish a baseline understanding of network assets and normal network traffic volume and flow
	Assess risks to network assets
	Obtain internal information on network operations via technical tools and user reports
	Obtain external information on threats, vulnerabilities, and incidents
	Detect anomalous activities
Analysis	Verify that an anomaly is an incident (threat of attack or actual attack)
	Investigate the incident to identify the type of cyber attack, estimate impact, and collect evidence
	Identify possible actions to mitigate the impact of the incident
	Integrate results into predictive analysis of broader implications or potential future attack
Warning	Develop attack and other notifications that are targeted and actionable
	Provide notifications in a timely manner
	Distribute notifications using appropriate communications methods

Table 1. (Continued).

Capability	Attribute
Response	Contain and mitigate the incident
	Recover from damages and remediate vulnerabilities
	Evaluate actions and incorporate lessons learned

Source: GAO analysis.

While US-CERT's cyber analysis and warning capabilities include aspects of each of the key attributes, they do not fully incorporate all of them. For example, as part of its monitoring, US-CERT obtains information from numerous external information sources; however, it has not established a comprehensive baseline of our nation's critical computer-reliant critical assets and network operations. In addition, while it investigates if identified anomalies constitute actual cyber threats or attacks as part of its analysis, the organization does not integrate its work into predictive analyses, nor does it have the analytical or technical resources to analyze multiple, simultaneous cyber incidents. The organization also provides warnings by developing and distributing a wide array of attack and other notifications; however, these notifications are not consistently actionable or timely—providing the right information to the right persons or groups as early as possible to give them time to take appropriate action. Further, while it responds to a limited number of affected entities in their efforts to contain and mitigate an attack, recover from damages, and remediate vulnerabilities, the organization does not possess the resources to handle multiple events across the nation.

US-CERT faces a number of newly identified and ongoing challenges that impede it from fully implementing the key attributes and in turn establishing cyber analysis and warning capabilities essential to coordinating the national effort to prepare for, prevent, and respond to cyber threats. The newly identified challenge is creating warnings that are actionable and timely—US-CERT does not consistently issue warning and other notifications that its customers find useful. Ongoing challenges that we previously identified and made recommendations to address are

- employing predictive cyber analysis—the organization has not established the ability to determine broader implications from ongoing network activity, predict or protect against future threats, or identify emerging attack methods;
- developing more trusted relationships to encourage information sharing— federal and nonfederal entities are reluctant to share information because US-CERT and these parties have yet to develop close working and trusted relationships that would allow the free flow of information;

- having sufficient analytical and technical capabilities—the organization has difficulty hiring and retaining adequately trained staff and acquiring supporting technology tools to handle a steadily increasing workload; and
- operating without organizational stability and leadership within DHS—the department has not provided the sustained leadership to make cyber analysis and warning a priority. This is due in part to frequent turnover in key management positions that currently also remain vacant. In addition, US-CERT's role as the central provider of cyber analysis and warning may be diminished by the creation of a new DHS center at a higher organizational level.

Until DHS addresses these challenges and fully incorporates all key attributes into its capabilities, it will not have the full complement of cyber analysis and warning capabilities essential to effectively performing its national mission.

Accordingly, we are making 10 recommendations to the Secretary of Homeland Security to improve DHS's cyber analysis and warning capabilities by implementing key cyber analysis and warning attributes and addressing the challenges, including

- developing close working and more trusted relationships with federal and nonfederal entities that would allow the free flow of information,
- expeditiously hiring sufficiently trained staff and acquiring supporting technology tools to handle the steadily increasing workload,
- ensuring consistent notifications that are actionable and timely,
- filling key management positions to provide organizational stability and leadership, and
- ensuring that there are distinct and transparent lines of authority and responsibility assigned to DHS organizations with cybersecurity roles and responsibilities.

In written comments on a draft of this chapter (see app. II), the department concurred with 9 of our 10 recommendations. It also described actions planned and under way to implement these recommendations. DHS took exception to 1 recommendation, stating that it had developed a conceptof-operations document that clearly defined roles and responsibilities for key DHS organizations. However, this document is still in draft, and the department has yet to establish a date for it to be finalized and implemented.

BACKGROUND

Increasing computer interconnectivity—most notably growth in the use of the Internet—has revolutionized the way that our government, our nation, and much of the world communicate and conduct business. While the benefits have been enormous, they are accompanied by significant risks to the nation's computer systems and to the critical operations and infrastructures that those systems support.[2]

Cyber Threats and Incidents Adversely Affect the Nation's Critical Infrastructure

Different types of cyber threats from numerous sources may adversely affect computers, software, a network, an agency's operations, an industry, or the Internet itself. Cyber threats can be unintentional or intentional. Unintentional threats can be caused by software upgrades or maintenance procedures that inadvertently disrupt systems. Intentional threats include both targeted and untargeted attacks. A targeted attack occurs when a group or individual specifically attacks a cyber asset. An untargeted attack occurs when the intended target of the attack is uncertain, such as when a virus, worm, or malware is released on the Internet with no specific target.

Threats to the Nation's Critical Infrastructure Are Proliferating

There is increasing concern among both government officials and industry experts regarding the potential for a cyber attack on the national critical infrastructure, including the infrastructure's control systems. The Department of Defense (DOD) and the Federal Bureau of Investigation, among others, have identified multiple sources of threats to our nation's critical infrastructure, including foreign nation states engaged in information warfare, domestic criminals, hackers, virus writers, and disgruntled employees working within an organization. In addition, there is concern about the growing vulnerabilities to our nation as the design, manufacture, and service of information technology have moved overseas.[3] For example, according to media reports, technology has been shipped to the United States from foreign countries with viruses on the storage devices.[4] Further, U.S. authorities are concerned about the prospect of combined physical and cyber attacks, which could have devastating consequences. For example, a cyber attack could disable a security system in order to facilitate a physical attack. Table 2 lists sources of threats that have been identified by the U.S. intelligence community and others.

Table 2. Sources of Emerging Cybersecurity Threats

Threat	Description
Bot-network operators	Bot-network operators take over multiple systems in order to coordinate attacks and to distribute phishing schemes, spam, and malware attacks (See table 3 for definitions). The services of these networks are sometimes made available on underground markets (e.g., purchasing a denial-of-service attack or servers to relay spam or phishing attacks).
Criminal groups	Criminal groups seek to attack systems for monetary gain. Specifically, organized crime groups are using spam, phishing, and spyware/malware to commit identity theft and online fraud. International corporate spies and organized crime organizations also pose a threat to the United States through their ability to conduct industrial espionage and large-scale monetary theft and to hire or develop hacker talent.
Foreign intelligence services	Foreign intelligence services use cyber tools as part of their information-gathering and espionage activities. In addition, several nations are aggressively working to develop information warfare doctrine, programs, and capabilities. Such capabilities enable a single entity to have a significant and serious impact by disrupting the supply, communications, and economic infrastructures that support military power—impacts that could affect the daily lives of U.S. citizens across the country.
Hackers	Hackers break into networks for the thrill of the challenge or for bragging rights in the hacker community. While gaining unauthorized access once required a fair amount of skill or computer knowledge, hackers can now download attack scripts and protocols from the Internet and launch them against victim sites. Thus, while attack tools have become more sophisticated, they have also become easier to use. According to the Central Intelligence Agency, the large majority of hackers do not have the requisite expertise to threaten difficult targets such as critical U.S. networks. Nevertheless, the worldwide population of hackers poses a relatively high threat of an isolated or brief disruption causing serious damage.
Insiders	The disgruntled organization insider is a principal source of computer crime. Insiders may not need a great deal of knowledge about computer intrusions because their knowledge of a target system often allows them to gain unrestricted access to cause damage to the system or to steal system data. The insider threat includes contractors hired by the organization as well as employees who accidentally introduce malware into systems.

Table 2. Sources of Emerging Cybersecurity Threats

Threat	Description
Phishers	Individuals, or small groups, execute phishing schemes in an attempt to steal identities or information for monetary gain. Phishers may also use spam and spyware/malware to accomplish their objectives.
Spammers	Individuals or organizations distribute unsolicited e-mail with hidden or false information in order to sell products, conduct phishing schemes, distribute spyware/malware, or attack organizations (i.e., denial of service).
Spyware/malware authors	Individuals or organizations with malicious intent carry out attacks against users by producing and distributing spyware and malware. Several destructive computer viruses and worms have harmed files and hard drives, including the Melissa Macro Virus, the Explore.Zip worm, the CIH (Chernobyl) Virus, Nimda, Code Red, Slammer, and Blaster.
Terrorists	Terrorists seek to destroy, incapacitate, or exploit critical infrastructures in order to threaten national security, cause mass casualties, weaken the U.S. economy, and damage public morale and confidence. Terrorists may use phishing schemes or spyware/malware in order to generate funds or gather sensitive information.

Source: GAO analysis based on data from the Federal Bureau of Investigation, the Central Intelligence Agency, and the Software Engineering Institute's CERT® Coordination Center.

The nation's critical infrastructure operates in an environment of increasing and dynamic threats, and adversaries are becoming more agile and sophisticated. Terrorists, transnational criminals, and intelligence services use various cyber tools that can deny access, degrade the integrity of, intercept, or destroy data and jeopardize the security of the nation's critical infrastructure (see table 3).

Table 3. Types of Cyber Attacks

Type of attack	Description
Denial of service	A method of attack from a single source that denies system access to legitimate users by overwhelming the target computer with messages and blocking legitimate traffic. It can prevent a system from being able to exchange data with other systems or use the Internet.
Distributed denial of service	A variant of the denial-of-service attack that uses a coordinated attack from a distributed system of computers rather than from a single source. It often makes use of worms to spread to multiple computers that can then attack the target.

Type of attack	Description
Exploit tools	Publicly available and sophisticated tools that intruders of various skill levels can use to determine vulnerabilities and gain entry into targeted systems.
Logic bombs	A form of sabotage in which a programmer inserts code that causes the program to perform a destructive action when some triggering event occurs, such as terminating the programmer's employment.
Phishing	The creation and use of e-mails and Web sites—designed to look like those of well-known legitimate businesses, financial institutions, and government agencies—in order to deceive Internet users into disclosing their personal data, such as bank and financial account information and passwords. The phishers then use that information for criminal purposes, such as identity theft and fraud.
Sniffer	Synonymous with packet sniffer. A program that intercepts routed data and examines each packet in search of specified information, such as passwords transmitted in clear text.
Trojan horse	A computer program that conceals harmful code. A Trojan horse usually masquerades as a useful program that a user would wish to execute.
Virus	A program that infects computer files, usually executable programs, by inserting a copy of itself into the file. These copies are usually executed when the infected file is loaded into memory, allowing the virus to infect other files. Unlike a computer worm, a virus requires human involvement (usually unwitting) to propagate.
Vishing	A method of phishing based on voice-over-Internet Protocol technology and open-source call center software that have made it inexpensive for scammers to set up phony call centers and criminals to send e-mail or text messages to potential victims, saying there has been a security problem and they need to call their bank to reactivate a credit or debit card, or send text messages to cell phones, instructing potential victims to contact fake online banks to renew their accounts.
War driving	A method of gaining entry into wireless computer networks using a laptop, antennas, and a wireless network adaptor that involves patrolling locations to gain unauthorized access.
Worm	An independent computer program that reproduces by copying itself from one system to another across a network. Unlike computer viruses, worms do not require human involvement to propagate.
Zero-day exploit	A cyber threat taking advantage of a security vulnerability on the same day that the vulnerability becomes known to the general public and for which there are no available fixes.

Source: GAO analysis of data from GAO and industry reports.

Cyber Incidents Have Caused Serious Damage

The growing number of known vulnerabilities increases the potential number of attacks. By exploiting software vulnerabilities, hackers and others who spread malicious code can cause significant damage, ranging from defacing Web sites to taking control of entire systems and thereby being able to read, modify, or delete sensitive information; disrupt operations; launch attacks against other organizations' systems; or destroy systems. Reports of attacks involving critical infrastructure demonstrate that a serious attack could be devastating, as the following examples illustrate.

- In June 2003, the U.S. government issued a warning concerning a virus that specifically targeted financial institutions. Experts said the BugBear.b virus was programmed to determine whether a victim had used an e-mail address for any of the roughly 1,300 financial institutions listed in the virus's code. If a match was found, the software attempted to collect and document user input by logging keystrokes and then provide this information to a hacker, who could use it in attempts to break into the banks' networks.[5]
- In August 2006, two Los Angeles city employees hacked into computers controlling the city's traffic lights and disrupted signal lights at four intersections, causing substantial backups and delays. The attacks were launched prior to an anticipated labor protest by the employees.[6]
- In October 2006, a foreign hacker penetrated security at a water filtering plant in Harrisburg, Pennsylvania. The intruder planted malicious software that was capable of affecting the plant's water treatment operations.[7]
- In May 2007, Estonia was the reported target of a denial-of-service cyber attack with national consequences. The coordinated attack created mass outages of its government and commercial Web sites.[8]
- In March 2008, the Department of Defense reported that in 2007 computer networks operated by Defense, other federal agencies, and defense-related think tanks and contractors were targets of cyber warfare intrusion techniques. Although those responsible were not definitively substantiated, the attacks appeared to have originated in China.[9]

As these examples illustrate, attacks resulting in the incapacitation or destruction of the nation's critical infrastructures could have a debilitating impact on national and economic security and on public health and safety.

Federal Law and Policy Establish the Need for National Cyber Analysis and Warning

To protect the nation's critical computer-dependent infrastructures against cyber threats and attacks, federal law and policy have identified the need to enhance cybersecurity and establish cyber analytical and warning capabilities, which are sometimes referred to as "indications and warnings." The laws and policies include (1) the Homeland Security Act of 2002, (2) the National Strategy to Secure Cyberspace, (3) Homeland Security Presidential Directive 7, and (4) the National Response Framework. In addition, the President issued in January 2008 Homeland Security Presidential Directive 23, which, according to US-CERT officials, has provisions that affect cyber analysis and warning efforts of the federal government.

Homeland Security Act of 2002

The Homeland Security Act of 2002 established the Department of Homeland Security and gave it lead responsibility for preventing terrorist attacks in the United States, reducing the vulnerability of the United States to terrorist attacks, and minimizing the damage and assisting in recovery from attacks that do occur.[10] The act assigned the department, among other things, a number of critical infrastructure protection responsibilities, including gathering of threat information, including cyber-related, from law enforcement, intelligence sources, and other agencies of the federal, state, and local governments and private sector entities to identify, assess, and understand threats; carrying out assessments of the vulnerabilities of key resources to determine the risks posed by attacks; and integrating information, analyses, and vulnerability assessments in order to identify priorities for protection. In addition, the department is responsible for disseminating, as appropriate, information that it analyzes—both within the department and to other federal, state, and local government agencies and private sector entities—to assist in the deterrence, prevention, preemption of, or response to terrorist acts.

National Strategy to Secure Cyberspace

The National Strategy to Secure Cyberspace proposes that a public/private architecture be provided for analyzing, warning, and managing incidents of national significance.[11] The strategy states that cyber analysis includes both (1) tactical analytical support during a cyber incident and (2) strategic analyses of threats. Tactical support involves providing current information on specific factors associated with incidents under investigation or specific identified vulnerabilities. Examples of tactical support include analysis of (1) a computer virus delivery mechanism to issue immediate guidance on ways to prevent or mitigate damage related to an imminent threat or (2) a specific computer intrusion or set of intrusions to determine the perpetrator, motive, and method of attack. Strategic analysis is predictive in that it looks beyond one specific incident to consider a broader set of incidents or implications that may indicate a potential future threat of national importance. For example, strategic analyses may identify long-term vulnerability and threat trends that provide advance warnings of increased risk, such as emerging attack methods. Strategic analyses are intended to provide policymakers with information that they can use to anticipate and prepare for attacks, thereby diminishing the damage from such attacks.

Homeland Security Presidential Directive 7

Homeland Security Presidential Directive 7 (HSPD 7) directs DHS to, among other things, serve as the focal point for securing cyberspace. This includes analysis, warning, information sharing, vulnerability reduction, mitigation, and recovery efforts for critical infrastructure information systems.[12] It also directs DHS to develop a national indications and warnings architecture for infrastructure protection and capabilities, including cyber, that will facilitate an understanding of baseline infrastructure operations, the identification of indicators and precursors to an attack, and create a surge capacity for detecting and analyzing patterns of potential attacks.

In May 2005, we reported that DHS has many cybersecurity-related roles and responsibilities, including developing and enhancing national cyber analysis and warning capabilities.[13] However, we found that DHS had not fully addressed all its cybersecurity-related responsibilities and that it faced challenges that impeded its ability to fulfill its responsibilities. These challenges included having organizational stability and authority, hiring employees, establishing information sharing and effective partnerships, and developing strategic analysis and warning. We made

recommendations to the Secretary of Homeland Security to engage appropriate stakeholders to prioritize key cybersecurity responsibilities, develop a prioritized list of key activities to addressing underlying challenges, and identify performance measures and milestones for fulfilling its responsibilities and for addressing its challenges. We did not make new recommendations regarding cyber-related analysis and warning because our previous recommendations had not been fully implemented. Specifically, in 2001, we recommended that responsible executive branch officials and agencies establish a capability for strategic analysis of computer-based threats, including developing a methodology, acquiring expertise, and obtaining infrastructure data.[14]

National Response Framework

The National Response Framework, issued by DHS in January 2008, provides guidance to coordinate cyber incident response among federal entities and, upon request, state and local governments and private sector entities.[15] Specifically, the Cyber Incident Annex describes the framework for federal cyber incident response in the event of a cyber-related incident of national significance affecting the critical national processes. Further, the annex formalizes the National Cyber Response Coordination Group (NCRCG). As established under the preceding National Response Plan, the NCRCG continues to be cochaired by DHS's National Cyber Security Division (NC SD), the Department of Justice's Computer Crime and Intellectual Property Section, and the DOD. It is to bring together officials from all agencies that have responsibility for cybersecurity and the sector- specific agencies identified in HSPD 7. The group coordinates intergovernmental and public/private preparedness and response to and recovery from national-level cyber incidents and physical attacks that have significant cyber-related consequences. During and in anticipation of such an incident, the NCRCG's senior-level membership is responsible for providing subject matter expertise, recommendations, and strategic policy support and ensuring that the full range of federal capabilities is deployed in a coordinated and effective fashion.

Homeland Security Presidential Directive 23

In January 2008, the President issued HSPD 23—also referred to as National Security Presidential Directive 54 and the President's "Cyber Initiative"—to improve the federal government's cybersecurity efforts, including protecting against intrusion attempts and better anticipating future threats.[16] While the directive is a classified document, US-CERT officials stated that it includes steps to enhance cyber analysis related efforts, such as requirements that federal agencies implement a centralized monitoring tool and that the federal government reduce the number of connections to the Internet, referred to as Trusted Internet Connections.

DHS Established US-CERT to Provide National Cyber Analysis and Warning

To help protect the nation's information infrastructure, DHS established the US-CERT. It is currently positioned within the NCSD of DHS's Office of Cybersecurity and Communications. Figure 1 shows the position of these offices within DHS's organizational structure.

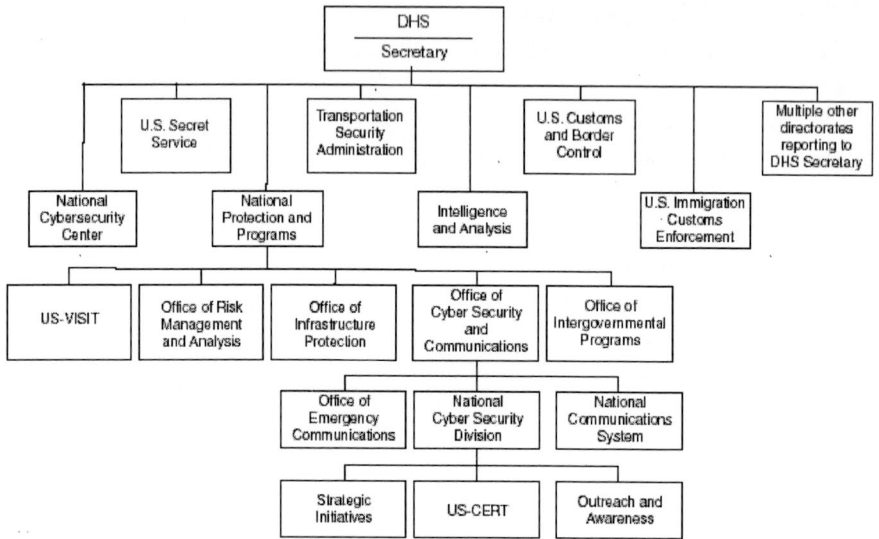

Source: GAO based on DHS data.

Figure 1. Department of Homeland Security Organizational Chart.

US-CERT is to serve as a focal point for the government's interaction with federal and nonfederal entities on a 24-hour-a-day, 7-day-a-week basis regarding cyber-related analysis, warning, information sharing, major incident response, and national-level recovery efforts.[17] It is charged with aggregating and disseminating cybersecurity information to improve warning of and response to incidents, increasing coordination of response information, reducing vulnerabilities, and enhancing prevention and protection. In addition, the organization is to collect incident reports from all federal agencies and assist agencies in their incident response efforts. It is also to accept incident reports when voluntarily submitted by other public and private entities and assist them in their response efforts, as requested.

US-CERT is composed of five branches, as shown in figure 2: Operations, Situational Awareness, Law Enforcement and Intelligence, Future Operations, and Mission Support. Each branch has specific responsibilities

- The Operations branch is to receive and respond to incidents, disseminate reasoned and actionable cybersecurity information, and analyze various types of data to improve overall understanding of current or emerging cyber threats affecting the nation's critical infrastructure.
- The Situational Awareness branch is to identify, analyze, and comprehend broad network activity and to support incident handling and analysis of

cybersecurity trends for federal agencies so that they may increase their own situational awareness and reduce cyber threats and vulnerabilities. As part of its responsibilities, the branch is responsible for managing the information garnered from the US-CERT Einstein program, which obtains network flow data from federal agencies, and analyzing the traffic patterns and behavior. This information is then combined with other relevant data to (1) detect potential deviations and identify how Internet activities are likely to affect federal agencies and (2) provide insight into the health of the Internet and into suspicious activities.

- The Law Enforcement and Intelligence branch is to facilitate information sharing and collaboration among law enforcement agencies, the intelligence community, and US-CERT through the presence of liaisons from those organizations at US-CERT.
- The Future Operations branch was established in January 2007 to lead or participate in the development of related policies, protocols, procedures, and plans to support US-CERT's coordination of national response to cyber incidents.
- The Mission Support branch is to manage US-CERT's communications mechanisms, including reports, alerts, notices, and its public and classified Web site content.

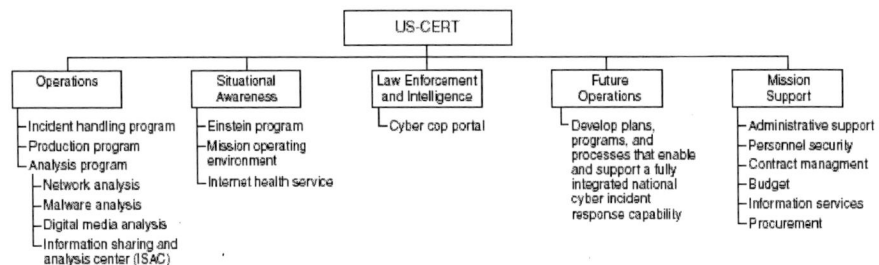

Source: GAO based on DHS data.

Figure 2. US-CERT Organizational Structure.

Cyber Analysis and Warning Encompasses Four Key Capabilities

Our research and observations at federal and nonfederal entities show that cyber analysis and warning typically encompasses four key capabilities:

- *Monitoring*—detecting cyber threats, attacks, and vulnerabilities and establishing a baseline of system and communication network assets and normal traffic.
- *Analysis*—using the information or intelligence gathered from monitoring to hypothesize about what the threat might be, investigate it with technical and contextual expertise and identify the threat and its impact, and determine possible mitigation steps. Analysis may be initiated in reaction to a detected anomaly. This is a tactical approach intended to triage information during a cyber incident and help make decisions. It may also be predictive, proactively reviewing data collected during monitoring to look at cyber events and the network environment to find trends, patterns, or anomaly correlations that indicate more serious attacks or future threats.
- *Warning*—developing and issuing informal and formal notifications that alert recipients in advance of potential or imminent, as well as ongoing, cyber threats or attacks. Warnings are intended to alert entities to the presence of cyber attack, help delineate the relevance and immediacy of cyber attacks, provide information on how to remediate vulnerabilities and mitigate incidents, or make overall statements about the health and welfare of the Internet.
- *Response*—taking actions to contain an incident, manage the protection of network operations, and recover from damages when vulnerabilities are revealed or when cyber incidents occur. In addition, response includes lessons learned and cyber threat data being documented and integrated back into the capabilities to improve overall cyber analysis and warning.

Through our consultations with experts, we found that the terminology may vary, but the functions of these capabilities are fairly consistent across cyber analysis and warning entities. Figure 3 depicts the basic process of cyber analysis and warning capabilities.

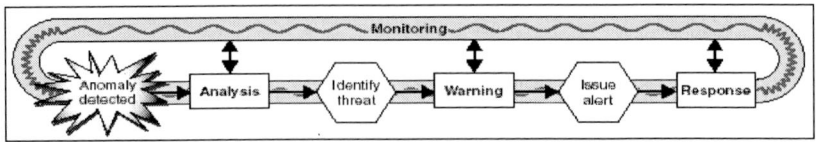

Source: GAO analysis.

Figure 3. A Simplified View of How Cyber Analysis and Warning Capabilities Are Executed.

Typically, cyber analysis and warning is executed, or managed, from a central focal point known as an operation center or watch center. Such centers can serve a single organization or a number of organizations. Centers generally include physically and electronically connected multidisciplinary teams with access to a variety of communication and software tools. The teams are made up of specialized analysts, sometimes referred to as watch standers, with a combination of expertise in information security, intelligence, and cyber forensics. Teams may also include subject area experts with specialized expertise in certain critical infrastructure sectors, industries, or technologies. The centers operate tools that integrate data and facilitate analysis by the watch standers. The data come from a multitude of sources, including internal or external monitoring, human or signals intelligence, analytical results, warnings from other entities, and information collected from previous threat responses. Centers decide when and how to issue formal and informal warnings that contribute to further analysis or provide information that aids in decisions about how to respond to an incident.

Depending on the size and organizational structure of an organization, the analysis and warning team may work with incident response teams during a cyber incident. The incident response team manages the decisions required for handling an incident using information discovered during monitoring, analysis, and warning. The team may also coordinate with those responsible for information security for the organization in order to assess risks, remediate vulnerabilities, and prepare for and respond to attacks.

FIFTEEN KEY ATTRIBUTES ESSENTIAL TO ESTABLISHING CYBER ANALYSIS AND WARNING CAPABILITIES

Our research and past experience at federal and nonfederal entities identified 15 key attributes associated with the cyber analysis and warning capabilities of monitoring, analysis, warning, and response. These attributes are displayed in table 4, which is followed by a detailed description by capability of each attribute.

Monitoring

Monitoring provides the data used to understand one's operating environment and detect changes that indicate the presence of anomalies that may be cyber attacks. It encompasses five key attributes:

Table 4. Key Attributes of the Cyber Analysis and Warning Capabilities

Capability	Attribute
Monitoring	Establish a baseline understanding of network assets and normal network traffic volume and flow Assess risks to network assets Obtain internal information on network operations via technical tools and user reports Obtain external information on threats, vulnerabilities, and incidents through various relationships, alerts, and other sources Detect anomalous activities
Analysis	Verify that an anomaly is an incident (threat of attack or actual attack) Investigate the incident to identify the type of cyber attack, estimate impact, and collect evidence Identify possible actions to mitigate the impact of the incident Integrate results into predictive analysis of broader implications or potential future attack
Warning	Develop attack and other notifications that are targeted and actionable Provide notifications in a timely manner Distribute notifications using appropriate communications methods
Response	Contain and mitigate the incident Recover from damages and remediate vulnerabilities Evaluate actions and incorporate lessons learned

Source: GAO analysis.

Monitoring

Monitoring provides the data used to understand one's operating environment and detect changes that indicate the presence of anomalies that may be cyber attacks. It encompasses five key attributes:

1. Establishing a baseline understanding of network assets and normal network traffic volume and flow

In order to detect unusual activity in network traffic or changes in an operating environment, organizations require knowledge of ordinary traffic and environmental conditions. This knowledge forms the baseline against which changes or anomalies can be detected, identified, and mitigated. A baseline is established through activities such as creating an accurate inventory of systems, prioritizing resources and assets, maintaining an understanding of the expected volume and nature of network traffic, and instituting operational procedures such as procedures for handling incidents. Without a baseline, it may be difficult to effectively detect threats or respond to a warning with the appropriate resources.

2. Assessing risks to network assets

Assessments should be conducted to determine what risks are posed by combinations of threats and vulnerabilities and inform the monitoring capability so that it is focused on the most critical assets. According to CERT® Coordination Center (CERT/CC) officials,[18] having a baseline knowledge of networks and systems and their associated risks in advance helps individual organizations understand what threats they may be susceptible to, what resources are at risk, and what the potential damage of an attack might be. Risks should be prioritized and mitigated until a reasonable acceptable level of risk is reached.

3. Obtain internal information on network operations via technical tools and user reports

Another key attribute is monitoring traffic on internal networks using (1) network and information security-related technology tools and (2) reports on network activity. As table 5 shows, various technologies can be used for internal network monitoring to help compile and identify patterns in network data. Each type of technology may detect anomalies that the other types of software cannot.

Table 5. Common Types of Technology Used for Internal Monitoring

Technology	Function
Antivirus software	Provides protection against malicious code, such as viruses, worms, and Trojan horses.
Firewalls	Control access to and from a network or computer.
Intrusion detection systems	Detect inappropriate, incorrect, or anomalous activity on a network or computer system.
Intrusion prevention systems	Build on intrusion detection systems to detect attacks on a network and take action to prevent them from being successful.
Signature-based tools	Compare files or packets to a list of "signatures"—patterns of specific files or packets that have been identified as a threat. Each signature is the unique arrangement of zeros and ones that make up the file.
Security event correlation tools	Monitor and document actions on network devices and analyze the actions to determine if an attack is ongoing or has occurred. Enable an organization to determine if ongoing system activities are operating according to its security policy.
Scanners	Analyze computers or networks for security vulnerabilities.

Source: GAO.

These technologies can be used to examine data logs from networks on a 24-hour-a-day, 7-day-a-week schedule in an effort to identify (1) precursors and indicators of cyber threats or other anomalies and (2) the occurrence of known attacks. The data logged from these technologies are typically prepared using automated tools to help analysts observe or detect a single anomaly or to discover patterns in data over time. According to several federal and nonfederal entities, hands-on monitoring by trained analysts is essential because it can be difficult for automated tools to identify anomalies and incidents. For example, some automated signature-based tools focus on known threats and may not automatically recognize or alert analysts to new attack patterns or new threat delivery techniques. Other intrusion detection systems can produce large numbers of alerts indicating a problem when one does not exist (false positives); therefore, an analyst must look into anomalies more closely to see if detected intrusions are indications of a threat or simply an equipment malfunction.

4. Obtaining external information on threats, vulnerabilities, and incidents through various relationships, alerts, and other sources

External monitoring includes observing and receiving information that is either publicly or not publicly available for the purpose of maintaining environmental or situational awareness, detecting anomalies, and providing data for analysis, warning, and response. External sources of information include

- formal relationships, such as with and between critical infrastructure sector-related information sharing and analysis centers (ISAC);[19] federal agencies, including military, civilian, law enforcement, and intelligence agencies; international computer emergency response team organizations; the CERT/CC and vendors under contract for services;
- informal relationships established on a personal basis between analysts located at different operations centers;
- alerts issued by federal, state, and local governments;
- alerts issued by commercial external sources such as network security and antivirus software vendors;
- vulnerability databases, standards, and frameworks such as the National Vulnerability Database,[20] the Common Vulnerability and Exposures List,[21] Common Vulnerability Scoring System,[22] and the Open Vulnerability Assessment Language;[23]
- media outlets, such as television news and newspapers; and

- Web sites, such as law enforcement entities' sites, known hacker and criminal sites and chat rooms, and cooperative cyber analysis and warning services.[24]

5. Detecting anomalous activities

Continuous monitoring occurs in order to detect significant changes from the baseline operations or the occurrence of an attack through an already known threat or vulnerability. It is ultimately the detection of an anomaly—observed internally or received from external information—and the recognition of its relevance that triggers analysis of the incident to begin.

Analysis

Analysis uses technical methods in combination with contextual expertise to hypothesize about the threat and associated risks concerning an anomaly and, if necessary, determine mitigation solutions. It encompasses four key attributes:

1. Verifying that an anomaly is an incident

Once an anomaly is detected, it should be verified whether it is a genuine cyber incident by determining that the data are from a trusted source and are accurate. For example, if the anomaly was identified by an internal sensor, analysts start by confirming that the sensor was working correctly and not indicating a false positive. If the anomaly was reported by an external source, analysts try to determine the trustworthiness of that source and begin to identify internal and external corroborating sources. Anomalies that are verified may require in-depth investigation and incident handling or more observation through monitoring.

2. Investigating the incident to identify the type of cyber attack, estimate impacts, and collect evidence

Once the anomaly is verified as a potential, impending, or occurring incident, analysts should combine information from multiple sources and/or perform investigative testing using available tools. Analysis often occurs through collaboration between analysts, the exchange of notifications and warnings, and the use of analytical research techniques. Analysts use these techniques to investigate the type of attack, its source (where it originates), its target (whom it affects), and the immediate risk to network assets and mission performance. In addition, these techniques are used to compile evidence for law enforcement. Techniques for investigation include

- comparing and correlating additional monitoring data available with the anomaly to determine what other internal and external entities are experiencing;
- comparing data about the anomaly with standardized databases to determine if the threats are known; and
- performing investigations, such as cyber forensic examinations,[25] reverse engineering, malware analysis, and isolating anomalies in a test environment such as a honeypot or a sandbox.[26]

3. Identifying possible actions to mitigate the impact of the incident

Analysis should culminate in identifying essential details about an anomaly such as what specific vulnerabilities are exploited or what impacts are expected for a specific incident. Steps should then be taken to identify alternative courses of action to mitigate the risks of the incident according to the severity of the exploit, available resources, and mission priorities. Such steps may include isolating the affected system to prevent further compromise, disabling the affected service that is being exploited, or blocking the connections providing the attacker a route into the network environment.[27] These courses of action may lead to more analysis or be used to support the warning capability.

4. Integrating results into predictive analysis of broader implications or potential future attacks

Information resulting from analysis of an individual incident should be used to determine any broader implications and predict and protect against future threats. This type of effort, or predictive analysis, should look beyond one specific incident to consider a broader set of incidents or implications that may indicate a potential threat of importance. For example, it may include detailed trend analysis of threats that have occurred over a certain period of time that is issued in public reports that discuss current trends, predict future incident activity, or emerging attack methods. However, according to many experts, this type of predictive analysis is complex and it is still difficult to predict future threats with current data.

Warning

Warnings are intended to alert entities to the presence of anomalies, help delineate the relevancy and immediacy of cyber attacks, provide information on how to remediate vulnerabilities and mitigate incidents, or make overall statements about the health and welfare of the Internet. Warning includes three key attributes:

1. Developing notifications that are targeted and actionable

Warning messages should be targeted to the appropriate audience and provide details that are accurate, specific, and relevant enough to be acted upon. Developing actionable notifications requires providing the right incident information to the right person or group. If a single group is the only target of a threat, a warning directly to it may be more appropriate than a general public announcement. In addition, warnings are tailored to address technical or nontechnical recipients. Some warnings may be more appropriate for chief information officers, while other may include technical details for network administrators. Although notifications and warnings are delivered throughout incident handling, it is important to reach a balance between releasing actionable information and disclosing warnings too often, which can overwhelm the recipients and stretch limited resources. By addressing the specific audience, warnings avoid overwhelming recipients with extraneous or irrelevant information.

Also, recipients of notifications and warnings need to be able to use them to protect or defend their networks against cyber attacks. For example, many organizations have designated thresholds that determine how and when warnings are issued. To do so, the messages must include specific and accurate information about the incident as it relates to the recipient's monitoring, analysis, or response capabilities. An actionable warning may also include recommendations about how to respond to an incident. Federal and nonfederal entities also noted that sensitivity of information and privacy are key considerations when trying to develop an actionable warning. Warnings are sanitized or stripped of identifying or proprietary information in order to protect the privacy of individuals or entities involved in the incident. In addition, the federal government and its private sector partners must also adhere to procedures to make sure that they share useful information at the appropriate clearance level.

2. Providing notifications in a timely manner

Warnings are intended to give information to recipients as early as possible—preferably in advance of a cyber attack—to give them time to take appropriate action. In addition, the National Institute of Standards and Technology (NIST) provides guidance to federal agencies that describes when incidents are considered reportable and how long they may take to report them to US-CERT.[28] Similarly, several ISACs stated that they have procedures that determine when and how warnings are issued and when and how members should report incidents.

3. Distributing notifications using the most appropriate communications methods

Once a warning is developed, it is important to determine the best method for getting that message out without overwhelming the public or incident handlers. Warnings can be provided both informally and formally. Informal warnings between colleagues with established trusted relationships can happen quickly and without significant regard to the organizational structure. Formal warnings, which are typically held to a higher standard of accuracy by recipients than informal warnings, come in many forms, such as e-mail bulletins, vulnerability alerts, Web postings, targeted warnings to a specific entity, or broad security notices to the general public. In addition to specific formal warnings, operations centers that perform analysis and warning for multiple organizations, such as the ISACs and commercial vendors, use level-based or color-coded alert systems on their Web sites to quickly notify members and the public of the general threat status of the infrastructure or Internet. Changing from one level or color to another indicates that the threat level is increasing or decreasing. These same organizations send alerts about threats and vulnerabilities to members only or may issue specific warnings to a single organization that has been identified through analysis as being targeted by a cyber threat.

Response

Response includes actions to contain an incident, manage the protection of network operations, and recover from damages when vulnerabilities are revealed or when cyber incidents occur. It encompasses three key attributes:

1. Containing and mitigating the incident

When an incident is identified, immediate steps should be taken to protect network assets. Decisions are made to control further impacts on the network and then eliminate the threat. These actions may include installing a software patch, blocking a port known to be used by a particular threat, or deploying other appropriate network resources. In the case of a serious threat, the decision may be to turn off the network gateway and temporarily isolate the network from the Internet, depending upon what assets are at risk. One industry expert noted that investigation may occur before any mitigation steps are taken in order to consider the necessity of law enforcement involvement. On the other hand, if little is known about a threat and it does not appear to endanger critical assets, a decision might be made to watch the threat emerge in a contained area to allow for further monitoring and analysis. Decisions to act or not are based on acceptable risks, available resources, and ability to remedy the known threat. In addition, decisions must be made in the context of the impact that actions will have on other related efforts, such as a law enforcement investigation.

2. Recovering from damage and remediating vulnerabilities

Once an incident is contained and mitigated, restoring damaged areas of the network to return it to its baseline becomes a priority. To understand the damage, a cyber damage or loss assessment may be conducted to identify, among other things, how the incident was discovered, what network(s) were affected, when the incident occurred, who attacked the network and by what methods, what was the intention of the attacker, what occurred during the attack, and what is the impact or severity of the incident. The recovery efforts may involve restoring or reinstalling computers, network devices, applications, or systems that have been compromised.

Taking action to remediate vulnerabilities in a network may also result from analysis and incident management. Entities work to discover and reduce the number of vulnerabilities in their computers, network devices, applications, or systems.

3. Evaluating actions and incorporating lessons learned

Entities should ensure that threat data, results, and lessons learned are evaluated and appropriately incorporated to improve the overall cyber analysis and warning capability. For example, teams can be used to simulate network threats by purposefully attacking a network in order to see how the network responds. From these simulations, an evaluation can be made about the response, and recommendations on how to improve can be developed. In addition, cyber simulations allow critical infrastructure organizations to prepare for threat scenarios and to test analysis, warning, and response capabilities. NIST guidance also states that holding lessons learned meetings after major incidents is helpful in improving security measures and the incident handling process itself.[29]

US-CERT's CAPABILITIES INCLUDE SOME BUT NOT ALL ASPECTS OF KEY ATTRIBUTES

US-CERT has established cyber analysis and warning capabilities that include aspects of each of the key attributes. However, they do not fully incorporate all of them.

Monitoring Capability Includes Most but Not All Aspects of Key Attributes

US-CERT has established capabilities that include aspects of key attributes of monitoring. For example, it obtains internal network operation information via technical tools and Einstein; obtains external information on threats, vulnerabilities, and incidents; and detects anomalous activities based on the information it receives. However, its capabilities do not fully incorporate all of the key attributes of monitoring. For example, it has not established a baseline of our nation's critical infrastructure information systems. Table 6 shows our analysis of its monitoring capability.

As part of the President's Cyber Initiative, DHS has a lead role for several provisions that, if implemented appropriately, could address key monitoring deficiencies, such as not having a comprehensive national baseline and sufficient external information on threats, vulnerabilities, and incidents. According to testimony by the Under Secretary for the National Protection and Programs Directorate, the initiative makes the Einstein program mandatory across all federal agencies. In addition, DHS plans to enhance Einstein's capabilities to be a real-time intrusion detection and situational awareness system. Further, DHS, along with the Office of Management and Budget (OMB), is responsible for working with federal agencies to reduce the number of Trusted Internet Connections used by the federal government. According to DHS and OMB officials, these initiatives will enhance the ability of the US-CERT to monitor federal systems for cyber attacks and other threats. According to US-CERT officials, the reduction in Trusted Internet Connections, along with the positioning of Einstein in front of those connections to the Internet, will help provide a governmentwide baseline and view of the traffic entering and leaving federal networks as well as access to the content of the traffic. In addition, according to the Assistant Secretary for Cybersecurity and Communications, the recently announced National Cybersecurity Center, which reports directly to the Secretary of Homeland Security, will be responsible for ensuring coordination among the cyber-related efforts across the federal government, including improving the sharing of incident and threat information. However, the efforts to use Einstein, reduce Internet connections, and implement the National Cybersecurity Center are in their early stages and have not yet been fully planned or implemented, so whether these efforts will fully address all five of the monitoring attributes is not known at this time.

Analysis Capability Does Not Fully Incorporate All Aspects of Key Attributes

US-CERT has established capabilities that include key attributes of analysis. For example, it verifies anomalies, performs investigations, and identifies possible courses of action. However, its capabilities do not fully incorporate other attributes because of technical and human resource constraints and the gaps in the monitoring capability. Table 8 shows our analysis of the organization's analysis capability.

As part of the Cyber Initiative, the organization has received additional resources to develop the next version of the Einstein situational awareness tool. According to US-CERT officials, this new version, referred to as Einstein 2.0, will provide real-time intrusion detection monitoring, a content analysis capability, and automated analysis functions that are currently manual. In addition, it has received authorization for an additional 30 government and 50 contractor employee full-time equivalents. According to US-CERT officials, they plan to fill the additional positions by leveraging graduates of the Scholarship for Service program, which provides cybersecurity-related scholarships to students willing to serve the federal government for a time commitment. However, these efforts are in their early stages and have not yet been fully planned or implemented. Consequently, whether these efforts will fully address all four of the analysis attributes is not known at this time.

Warning Capability Exhibits Some but Not All Characteristics of Key Attributes

The organization has established capabilities that include key attributes of warning. For example, it develops and distributes a number of attack and other notifications targeted to different audiences with varying frequency. However, according to customers, these warning products are not consistently actionable and timely. Table 8 shows our analysis of the organization's warning capability. Tables 9 and 10 show types of warning products and the quantity of products issued during fiscal year 2007.

Table 6. US-CERT Capabilities Includes Most but Not All Aspects of Monitoring

Attribute	Aspects incorporated	Aspects not incorporated
Establish a baseline understanding of network assets and normal network traffic volume and flow	The organization has a limited baseline understanding of network assets and normal network traffic volume through the 16 federal participants in its situational awareness tool, USCERT Einstein. In addition, it receives additional network flow information through contracts with information security vendors.	It does not have a comprehensive national-level baseline across the nation's computer-reliant critical infrastructure, including the information systems of federal civilian and military entities, state and local governments, the private sector, and other entities. For example, under Einstein, the organization monitors 16 agencies, a practice that does not provide an overall view of federal network traffic. In addition, the tool's current capabilities are manually driven, thereby complicating and slowing the collection and compilation of data.
Assess risks to network assets	—	Though US-CERT is involved in cyber-related risk assessment efforts being performed by other DHS organizations and the private sector, it does not perform risk assessments.
Obtain internal information on network operations via technical tools and user reports	The organization obtains internal information using security tools and user reports regarding its presence on the Internet and its internal network operations.	Its ability to obtain real-time internal traffic information is reduced by Einstein's limitation of requiring manually intensive analysis.

Attribute	Aspects incorporated	Aspects not incorporated
Obtain external information on threats, vulnerabilities, and incidents.	US-CERT monitors a variety of external information sources, including network traffic data, incident reports, and threat reports from federal, state, local, and foreign governments and the private sector, such as the following: • federal agencies providing an enhanced view of their networks through participation in Einstein; • various vendors providing Internet operational data; • the Homeland Infrastructure Threat and Risk Analysis Center (HITRAC), a law enforcement, and the intelligence community, providing threat information and other data; • federal agencies reporting information security incidents to the organization, as required by the Federal Information Security Management Act;b • nonfederal entities voluntarily reporting incidents, malware, and other information; • foreign governments providing information on cyber incidents; • CERT/CC providing vulnerability information; and • other analysis and warning entities, including the Financial Services-ISAC, Multistate ISAC, the Internet Storm Center, and information security vendors, sharing incident and other situational awareness information.	Its information does not encompass all critical infrastructure information networks. For example, by monitoring only 16 agencies, Einstein does not provide an overall view of federal network traffic. Also, the Department of Energy and DOD use their own similar situational awareness tools, but their data are not currently combined with Einstein's data to provide a more complete view of federal traffic. There are efforts under way to develop automated information exchanges between DOD's system and Einstein, but as of March 2008, this had not been finalized. Regarding nonfederal entities, the organization does not directly monitor any private sector networks, nor are nonfederal entities required to report to it incidents or anomalous activity. Typically, nonfederal entities, including the ISACs, that report incident and other data filter sensitive details from the data reported.

Table 6. (Continued).

Attribute	Aspects incorporated	Aspects not incorporated
Detect anomalous activities.	The organization detects anomalies based on its monitoring of network traffic flow. Einstein provides network flow data from 16 agencies with the primary goal of looking for unique activity that may indicate a cyber attack or other undesirable activity.[c] According to US-CERT officials, Einstein provides the participating agencies a capability to compare their network traffic data with activity at other federal agencies and against law enforcement and intelligence agencies' threat data to determine if they are the victim of serious attacks. In addition, it works with its various partners in the private sector as well as other federal, state, and local governments to determine the extent of abnormal behavior. For example, the organization receives limited information from certain computer security vendors regarding Internet traffic flow of their respective customer bases.	The organization does not detect anomalies across the nation's computer-reliant critical infrastructure. For example, it does not directly monitor any private sector networks, nor are nonfederal entities required to report incidents or anomalous activity.

Source: GAO analysis.

[a]HITRAC is a fusion center of intelligence analysts from DHS's Office of Intelligence and Analysis and subject matter experts from the National Protection and Programs Directorate working together to analyze threats, vulnerabilities, and risks to the 18 Critical Infrastructure/Key Resource sectors of the United States. Additionally, HITRAC focuses solely on analyzing and identifying the threat aspect of cybersecurity incidents as they occur. HITRAC shares these threat data with numerous customers, including US-CERT.

[b]The Federal Information Security Management Act requires the operation of a central federal information security incident center. 44 U.S.C. 3546. The act also requires agencies to report incidents to the organization, in addition to law enforcement agencies, relevant offices of inspector general, and other designated entities. 44 U.S.C. 3544(b)(7).

[c]These data are analyzed for traffic patterns and behavior; this information can be combined with other relevant data to (1) detect potential deviations and identify how Internet activities are likely to affect federal agencies and (2) provide insight into the health of the Internet and suspicious activities.

Table 7. US-CERT Incorporates Some but Not All Aspects of Analysis

Attribute	Aspects incorporated	Aspects not incorporated
Verify that an anomaly is an incident (threat of attack or actual attack)	When an anomaly is detected or reported, USCERT works directly with its various public and private sector partners to determine whether the anomaly is an incident. For example, it notifies federal agencies when it observes abnormal activities. In turn, federal agencies take the information provided and are to verify whether the activity constitutes a cybersecurity incident and if any support is required from US-CERT.	The lack of a robust monitoring capability negatively affects the organization's ability to verify and investigate anomalies and to identify threats. Specifically, although the Einstein flow data are collected in real time, the actual analysis is manually intensive and does not occur simultaneously or in real time. Another limiting factor of Einstein data is that the organization is unable to analyze the content of the potentially malicious traffic.
Investigate the incident to identify the type of cyber attack, estimate impacts, and collect evidence	The organization investigates incidents through network and malware analysis. For example, it correlates Einstein network traffic data with known vulnerabilities and threats to identify abnormal activity, and then it focuses on identifying emerging threats, ongoing trends, and intrusions that have already occurred. According to agency officials, the amount of time needed to discover and understand a potential cyber attack and communicate it to agencies has been significantly reduced from 4 to 5 days to 4 to 5 hours. In addition, according to USCERT officials, its malware analysis focuses on reverse engineering malicious code to determine how the code works, its effect on a network or system, and potentially who developed it. The organization receives the malware code from a variety of sources, including its own monitoring, anonymous submissions, and formal submissions from affected entities, such as federal agencies, Internet service providers, and other entities.	The number of incidents that can be analyzed at one time is limited.

Table 7. (Continued).

Attribute	Aspects incorporated	Aspects not incorporated
	For example, according to agency officials, they receive on average between 5,000 and 24,000 individual pieces of malware in a 24-hour period. Additionally as of April 2008, officials stated that the organization had conducted analysis on 1,520,022 samples of malware code during fiscal year 2008. To do this work, the organization has established a segregated facility, or malware laboratory, that provides a controlled environment to conduct detailed analysis on infected computer hardware and software. According to officials, its malware capability has provided value to federal and nonfederal partners because it can analyze the potential impact of malware with the known threat information received from its partners in the law enforcement and intelligence communities.	
Identify possible actions to mitigate the impact of the incident	US-CERT's analysts develop alternative actions for stopping or controlling the threat. These alternatives are based on risk, required resources, mission priorities, and existing network requirements and limitations. Its network analysts work with all US-CERT partners to identify possible courses of action and methods to respond to cyber incidents. For example, in January 2008, an analysis of malware discovered at a targeted federal agency led to the identification of three zero-day exploits and a subsequent alert issued to federal and nonfederal entities.	The organization's ability to develop possible actions to mitigate the identified threat is limited by its inability to engage other partners in analysis efforts because the information may be sensitive or classified.
Integrate results into predictive analysis of broader implications or potential future attack	According to NCSD officials, the organization is engaged in activities with other NCSD entities to develop more strategic views of the nation's critical cyber infrastructures.	The organization does not possess the capability to integrate its work into predictive analysis.

Source: GAO analysis.

Table 8. US-CERT Exhibits Some but Not All Aspects of Warning

Attribute	Aspects incorporated	Aspects not incorporated
Develop attack and other notifications that are targeted and actionable	As tables 9 and 10 depict, the organization develops various attack and other notifications for a varied set of customers.	Officials from entities with robust cyber analysis and warning capabilities, such as the ISACs, DOD, and the Department of Energy, stated that the organization's notifications typically did not offer new or additional information beyond their own efforts.
Provide notifications in a timely manner	The organization is occasionally able to provide notifications to certain customers in a timely manner. For example, officials from organizations with limited cyber analysis and warning capabilities stated that certain US-CERT notifications, especially those warnings with For Official Use Only (FOUO) information, were extremely timely.	The organization is not consistently able to provide notifications in a timely manner. Its ability to disseminate timely notifications is hindered by a number of factors. First, as the national cyber analysis and warning organization, it must ensure a high level of accuracy in the products it releases. In order to avoid disseminating incomplete or inaccurate information, its warning products are subjected to a review process, which can prevent their rapid dissemination. Further, the sensitivity of information can be a hindrance. Specifically, highly sensitive information must be coordinated with other components as part of the review process, which can add days to the release time. Finally, dissemination efforts are limited by lack of performance measures that assess or provide feedback on the value of US-CERT products.
Distribute notifications using appropriate communications methods	As table 9 depicts, the organization distributes a wide array of attack and other "warning" products through various mechanisms to a diverse set of customers.	According to NSCD officials, the organization is refining its distribution lists and collaborating with various federal and nonfederal user groups to better ensure appropriate officials (those having the understanding and ability to appropriately respond) receive its notifications.

Source: GAO analysis.

Table 9. US-CERT Warning Products, Fiscal Year 2007

US-CERT products	Product audience					
	White House	Federal government	GFIRST[a]	Select international partners[b]	ISACs[c]	General public
Situational awareness report	*		*	*	*	
Federal information notice	*	*	*			
Critical infrastructure information notice	*			*	*	
Public trends and analysis report		*	*	*	*	*
Technical information paper	*	*	*	*	*	*
Cyber daily briefing			*		*	
Non-technical alerts						*
Technical alerts	*	*	*	*	*	*
Security bulletins	*	*	*	*	*	*
Security tips						*
Current activity	*	*	*	*	*	*
Vulnerability notes	*	*	*	*	*	*

[a] Government Forum of Incident Response and Security Teams (GFIRST) is a group of technical and tactical practitioners from government agency security response teams responsible for securing government information technology systems.

[b] Select international partners including Australia, Canada, New Zealand, and the United Kingdom.

[c] Information sharing and analysis center.

[d] Homeland Secure Data Network (HSDN) is a secure portal that provides the ability to share information at the Secret category level among other federal, state, and local government entities.

[e] DHS considers the Homeland Security Information Network (HSIN) to be its primary communication application for transmitting sensitive but unclassified information.

According to DHS, this network is an encrypted, unclassified, Web-based communications application that serves as DHS's primary nationwide information-sharing and collaboration tool. It is intended to offer both real-time chat and instant messaging capability, as well as a document library that contains reports from multiple federal, state, and local sources.

[f] DHS established the National Cyber Alert System (NCAS) to deliver targeted, timely, and actionable information to the public on how to secure computer systems. Information provided by the alert system is designed to be understandable by all computer users, both technical and nontechnical.

[g] Really Simple Syndication (RSS) is a format for gathering and making available content from Web sites. RSS can be used to provide any kind of information that can be broken down into discrete items and put into RSS format, typically called an RSS feed. Software is available that can periodically check RSS feeds for changes, download new items, and make them available to the users.

Table 10. Quantity of US-CERT Warning Products, Fiscal Year 2007

Product	Quantity	Interval
Public trends and analysis reports	4	Quarterly
Vulnerability notes	353	As needed
Situational awareness reports (SAR)	83	As needed
Federal information notices (FIN)	7	As needed
Technical information papers (TIP)	8	As needed
Critical infrastructure information notices (CIIN)	9	As needed
Security bulletins	52	Weekly
Technical alerts	39	As needed
Nontechnical alerts	27	As needed
Current activity	260	As needed
Cyber daily briefings	356	Daily

As part of the Cyber Initiative, the enhancements to the Einstein program, as well as the reduction in the number of Trusted Internet Connections can lead to more complete data. According to US-CERT officials, the improved data will lead to an enhanced warning capability that could provide the ability to issue targeted and actionable alerts in advance of actual cyber attacks. However, these efforts are in their early stages and have not yet been fully planned or implemented; thus, it is not clear whether these efforts will fully address the three warning attributes.

Response Capability Satisfies Some but Not All Aspects of Key Attributes

US-CERT possesses a limited response capability to assist other entities in the containment, mitigation, and recovery from significant cyber incidents. For example, while it provides on-site assistance to various entities, its ability to provide response at the national level is hindered by limitations in the resources available and authority over affected entities. Table 11 shows our analysis of its response capability.

To improve the organization's response capability, US-CERT officials stated that they needed to perform internal exercises that test its national-level response capability more often than every 2 years, as is the case with the Cyber Storm exercise.[30] It plans to develop "tabletop" exercises to more frequently test its response capabilities. In addition, according to NCSD officials, they are working collaboratively with other federal and nonfederal working groups to improve their performance measures so that they can understand the value and use of their products and make continuous improvements. However, until they do so, it is not clear whether these efforts will lead to US-CERT fully addressing the three response attributes.

US-CERT FACES NEW AND ONGOING CHALLENGES TO FULFILLING ITS MISSION

US-CERT faces a number of newly identified and ongoing challenges that impede it from fully implementing the key attributes and in turn establishing cyber analysis and warning capabilities essential to coordinating the national effort to prepare for, prevent, and respond to cyber threats. The new challenge is creating warnings that are actionable and timely—it does not consistently issue warning and other notifications that its customers find useful. In addition, US-CERT continues to face four challenges that we previously identified: (1) employing predictive cyber analysis, (2) developing more trusted relationships to encourage information sharing, (3) having sufficient analytical and technical capabilities, and (4) operating without organizational stability and leadership within DHS. Until DHS addresses these challenges and fully incorporates all key attributes into its capabilities, it will not have the full complement of cyber analysis and warning capabilities essential to effectively performing its national mission.

Table 11. US-CERT Satisfies Some but Not All Aspects of Response

Attribute	Aspects incorporated	Aspects not incorporated
Contain and mitigate the incident	The organization assists entities in federal, state, and local governments as well as the private sector with the containment and mitigation of cybersecurity incidents as they occur, on a requested basis. According to agency officials, the US-CERT routinely deploys its two digital media analysis teams to perform on-site response to serious incidents. These teams have the capabilities and depth of knowledge to perform detailed analysis on compromised media (e.g., hard drives and thumb drives). For example, as of April 2008, the organization had provided on-site incident response eight times for fiscal year 2008, making about 30 visits to various federal agencies to address incidents dealing with unauthorized access, malware activity, as well as misconfigured network devices. Also, in November 2007, the organization deployed at least one response team to each of five different federal agencies over 5 consecutive days. In addition, the Law Enforcement and Intelligence branch works with organizations such as the Federal Bureau of Investigation and United States Secret Service to contain incidents on a global scale using established relationships with other nations. According to officials, the organization has also assisted at the international level, most recently deploying officials to Estonia to help its government improve its cybersecurity posture after suffering a major cyber attack. Further, DHS, in conjunction with DOD and the Department of Justice, formed the NCRCG to coordinate the federal response to cyber incidents of national significance. During a significant national incident, the NCRCG is to provide subject matter expertise, recommendations, and strategic policy support to the Secretary of Homeland Security. At the time of our review, the senior-level membership had coordinated and communicated about incidents; however, there had not been a cyber incident of national significance to activate these procedures.	Though the organization is responsible for responding to national-level incidents, it does not possess the authority to compel an agency or organization to take action.

Recover from damages and remediate vulnerabilities	The organization routinely deploys its two digital media analysis teams to perform on-site response to serious incidents at federal agencies. According to agency officials, these teams focus on serious incidents, typically involving advanced threats, such as those propagated by nation states as well as advanced malware attacks.	To handle a cyber attack that affects multiple entities across the nation, officials stated that the organization would need at least three additional digital media analysis teams.
Evaluate actions and incorporate lessons learned	US-CERT has identified shortcomings in its processes, communications methods, and policies by conducting exercises that simulate a national-level incident. For example, once a digital media team has completed its on-site response assistance, it generates an after-action report that summarizes what steps were taken and any further suggested actions for the affected organization. In addition, during Cyber Storm II, which occurred in March 2008, the organization identified a number of issues for improvement that will be addressed in after-action reports and tracked to ensure changes occur.	While it measures certain items, such as the number and type of products it distributes, the organization has not established performance measures to determine the effectiveness of its efforts. According to US-CERT officials, other than an occasional statement of appreciation from other organizations, they do not know who benefits from their efforts or who uses their products.

New Challenge Involves Creating Warnings that Are Actionable and Timely

Developing and disseminating cyber threat warnings to enable customers to effectively mitigate a threat in advance of an attack can be challenging for the US-CERT. According to the organization's Acting Deputy Director, it serves as the nation's cyber analysis and warning center and must ensure that its warnings are accurate. In addition, owners of classified or law enforcement information must review and agree to the release of related information. Therefore, the organization's products are subjected to a stringent review and revision process that could adversely affect the timeliness of its products—potentially adding days to the release if classified or law enforcement information must be removed from the product. For example, an official from a cybersecurity-focused organization at a university stated that the alerts from US-CERT generally arrive a day or two after they might have been helpful. An official from another private entity stated that the bureaucratic process US-CERT must follow prevents it from providing useful alerts in a timely manner and that as a result, it does not have the credibility to drive a reaction when an alert is finally issued. Another private sector official stated that, in some cases, the organization gets information on cyber incidents and attacks faster from media sources than US-CERT because its analysts need time to verify the reliability of the data they receive.

In addition, according to federal officials responsible for determining cyber-related threats, US-CERT, as well as other organizations with cybersecurity-related responsibilities, must also balance the need to develop and release warnings with the activities of other organizations, such as law enforcement and intelligence support, to identify and mitigate cyber threats. For example, the release of a warning to address a threat or attack may also alert the intruders that their methods have been discovered and cause them to change their methods prior to the completion of an investigation about their activities.

Further, when there is sensitive information to share, US-CERT officials stated that on numerous occasions, they were unable to share the details of threats to customers' networks because no one within the federal agency or nonfederal entity possessed a security clearance high enough to receive the information. In some organizations, the individuals who do possess security clearances are in the upper echelons of the organization and do not possess a cyber or information security background. As a result, they are not always able to accurately comprehend and relay the threat information to those who would actually handle the mitigation efforts. In September 2007, we reported that DHS lacked a rapid, efficient process for disseminating sensitive information to private industry owners and operators of critical infrastructures.[31] We recommended that DHS establish a rapid and secure process for sharing sensitive vulnerability information with critical infrastructure stakeholders, including vendors, owners, and operators; however, DHS has not yet fulfilled this recommendation.

To provide actionable information to its customers, the organization attempts to combine incident information with related cyber threat information to determine the seriousness of the attack. However, according to the Acting Director of US-CERT, its efforts are limited by other federal entities' abilities to determine specific cyber threats to the nation's critical infrastructure. One reason for the lack of cyber threat data is that the task is complex and difficult and there are no established, generally accepted methodologies for performing such analysis. In addition, such entities are hampered by the limited number of analysts dedicated to cyber threat identification. For example, in January 2008, the Director of HITRAC stated that only 5 percent of HITRAC's total number of analyst positions was focused on analyzing and identifying cyber threats to our nation's critical information infrastructure. According to the director, it had received approval to double the number of cyber-related analysts and was in the process of filling those positions. In addition, the director stated that HITRAC's primary focus is on identifying physical threats.

Ongoing Challenges Involve Establishing Predictive Analysis, Trusted Relationships, Analytical and Technical Capabilities, and a Stable Organization

US-CERT faces ongoing challenges that we identified in previous reports as impeding DHS's ability to fulfill its cyber critical infrastructure protection responsibilities.

Employing predictive cyber analysis—US-CERT has been unable to establish the solid foundation needed to perform predictive cyber analysis that would enable it to determine any broader implications from ongoing network activity, predict or protect against future threats, or identify emerging attack methods prior to an attack. Since 2001, we have identified the challenges associated with establishing strategic, predictive analysis and warning and have made recommendations that responsible executive branch officials and agencies establish such capabilities, including developing methodologies.[32] According to the Acting Director of US-CERT, it has not been able to establish such capabilities because there is not a generally accepted methodology for performing predictive cyber analysis and warning. In addition, officials from US-CERT and other federal and nonfederal entities with cyber analysis and warning capabilities stated that while they can determine the motivations for the various threat sources to use cyber attacks, it is a formidable task to foresee prior to attacks how those threats would actually conduct attacks and to establish indicators to recognize that such cyber attacks are about to occur. Also, the relative newness of the cyber analysis and warning discipline and immaturity of the related methodologies and tools add to the complexity.

Developing more trusted relationships to encourage information sharing—Implementing cyber analysis and warning capabilities, including all of the key attributes, requires that entities be willing and able to share information, including details about incidents, threats, vulnerabilities, and network operations. However, US-CERT continues to be challenged to develop relationships with external sources that would encourage information sharing. For example, nonfederal entities do not consistently fully disclose incident and other data—they filter sensitive details from the data reported, thus reducing its value to US-CERT. The lack of such relationships negatively affects the organization's cyber analysis and warning capability.

In 2005, we reported that entities within critical infrastructure sectors possess an inherent disincentive to share cybersecurity information with DHS.[33] Much of their concern was that the potential release of sensitive information could increase the threat they face. In addition, when information was shared, it was not clear whether the information would be shared with other entities, such as other federal entities, state and local entities, law enforcement, or various regulators, or how it would be used or protected from disclosure. Alternatively, sector representatives expressed concerns that DHS was not effectively communicating information with them and had not matched private sector efforts to share valuable information with a corresponding level of trusted information sharing. We also identified information sharing in support of homeland security as a high-risk area in 2005, and we noted that establishing an effective two-way exchange of information to help detect, prevent, and mitigate potential terrorist attacks requires an extraordinary level of cooperation and perseverance among federal, state, and local governments and the private sector.[34]

Federal and nonfederal officials raised similar concerns about the ability to develop trusted relationships and share information with and between cyber analysis and warning entities, including US-CERT. For example, frequent staff turnover at NCSD and US-CERT hindered the ability to build trusted relationships with both public and private entities. Federal and nonfederal officials stated that reliance was placed on personal relationships to support sharing of sensitive information about cybersecurity and cyber incidents. However, according to the NCSD director, six senior staff members within the Office of Cybersecurity and Communications (the national focal point for addressing cybersecurity issues) were leaving for various reasons, affecting the ability to develop such relationships. In addition, private sector officials stated that their organizations continued to be hesitant to share information on vulnerabilities and threats because of the fear that such sharing might negatively affect their financial bottom line. For example, private sector officials stated that it was difficult to share unfiltered information with their respective infrastructure sector ISAC because a competitor operated the ISAC, thus negatively affecting the information received by US-CERT.

Having sufficient analytical and technical capabilities—Obtaining and retaining adequately trained cyber analysts and acquiring up-to-date technological tools to implement the analysis capability attributes is an ongoing challenge to US-CERT and other analysis and warning centers, hindering their ability to respond to increasingly fast, nimble, and sophisticated cyber attacks. As we have reported, NCSD has had difficulty hiring personnel to fill vacant positions.[35] We reported that once it found qualified candidates, some candidates decided not to apply or withdrew their applications because it took too long to be hired. This is still a concern because current staff has limited organizational backup and, in some cases, performs multiple roles. In addition, a private sector official stated that it is not clear whether or not the government has the number of technical analysts necessary to perform analysis on large and complex data sets that are generated whether or not an incident is in progress or not.

Keeping cyber analysts trained and up to date on the latest cybersecurity tools and techniques can be difficult. For example, a DOD official representing one of its cyber analysis and warning centers stated that its analysts must develop their expertise on the job because there is no formal training program available that teaches them how to detect and perform analysis of an anomaly or intrusion. A private sector official stated that while analysts are often trained to use existing tools, their understanding of the key attributes of analysis is often limited, resulting in a solution too late to be helpful.

Analysts also need the appropriate technological tools to handle the volume, velocity, and variety of malicious data and activity they are faced with, according to federal officials. For example, although the Einstein flow data are collected in real time, the actual analysis is manually intensive and does not occur simultaneously or in real time. Another limiting factor of Einstein data is that US-CERT is unable to analyze the content of the potentially malicious traffic and must rely on the affected agency to perform any analysis of the content of the traffic. Thus both the reaction time to determine the intent of the anomalous activity and the necessary actions to address it are significantly slowed. In addition, officials from one private sector entity questioned if agencies can sufficiently protect their networks using the tools they are mandated to use.

As part of the efforts to address the President's Cyber Initiative, US-CERT recently received approval to fill 80 new positions—30 government and 50 contractor—and is attempting to fill these analytical positions by extending offers to candidates in the National Science Foundation's Scholarship for Service Program. However, these positions have yet to be completely filled with qualified candidates.

Operating without organizational stability and authority—We have identified challenges regarding DHS's organizational stability, leadership, and authority that affect US-CERT's ability to successfully perform its mission. In the past, we have reported that the lack of stable leadership has diminished NC SD's ability to maintain trusted relationships with its infrastructure partners and has hindered its ability to adequately plan and execute activities.[36] While DHS has taken steps to fill key positions, organizational instability among cybersecurity officials continues to affect NCSD and thus US-CERT. For example, at least six senior staff members were leaving DHS's Office of Cybersecurity and Communications, including the NCSD Director. Losing senior staff members in such large numbers has negatively affected the agency's long-term planning and hampered the ability of NCSD/US-CERT to establish trusted relationships with public and private entities and to build adequate functions to carry out its mission, including expanded cyber analysis and warning capabilities, according to the official.

Furthermore, when new senior leadership has joined DHS, NCSD/US-CERT's objectives were reassessed and redirected, thus affecting NCSD's ability to have a consistent long-term strategy, according to the former official. For example, senior officials wanted to broaden the role and focus of US-CERT by having it provide centralized network monitoring for the entire federal government on a 24-hour-a-day, 7-day-aweek basis. However, the Director of NCSD disagreed with this strategy, stating that each federal agency should have its own 24-hour-a-day, 7-daya-week incident-handling capability (either in-house or contracted out) to respond to incidents affecting its own network. He viewed US-CERT as a fusion center that would provide analysis and warning for national-level incidents, support federal agency incident-handling capabilities during crisis situations, and offer a mechanism for federal agencies to coordinate with law enforcement.

The organization's future position in the government's efforts to establish a national-level cyber analysis and warning capability is uncertain. Specifically, Homeland Security Presidential Directive 23, which is classified, creates questions about US-CERT's future role as the focal point for national cyber analysis and warning. In addition, DHS established a new National Cybersecurity Center at a higher organizational level, which may diminish the Assistant Secretary of Cyber Security and Communications' authority as the focal point for the federal government's cybersecurity-related critical infrastructure protection efforts, and thus US-CERT's role as the central provider of cyber analysis and warning capabilities across federal and nonfederal critical infrastructure entities.

As stated above, we did not make new recommendations in 2005 regarding cyber analysis and warning because our previous recommendations had not yet been fully implemented. At the time, we did recommend that the Secretary of Homeland Security require NCSD to develop a prioritized list of key activities for addressing the underlying challenges related to information sharing, hiring staff with appropriate capabilities, and organizational stability and authority. In addition, we recommended that performance measures and milestones for performing activities to address these challenges be identified. However, since that time, DHS has not provided evidence that it has taken actions on these activities.

CONCLUSIONS

In seeking to counter the growing cyber threats to the nation's critical infrastructures, DHS has established a range of cyber analysis and warning capabilities, such as monitoring federal Internet traffic and the issuance of routine warnings to federal and nonfederal customers. However, while DHS has actions under way aimed at helping US-CERT better fulfill attributes identified as critical to demonstrating a capability, US-CERT still does not exhibit aspects of the attributes essential to having a truly national capability. It lacks a comprehensive baseline understanding of the nation's critical information infrastructure operations, does not monitor all critical infrastructure information systems, does not consistently provide actionable and timely warnings, and lacks the capacity to assist in mitigation and recovery in the event of multiple, simultaneous incidents of national significance.

Planned actions could help to mitigate deficiencies. For example, as part of the Cyber Initiative, US-CERT plans to enhance its Einstein situational awareness tool so that it has real-time intrusion detection monitoring, a content analysis capability, and automated analysis functions. By placing the tool in front of Trusted Internet Connections, officials expect to obtain a governmentwide baseline view of the traffic and content entering and leaving federal networks. US-CERT also plans to hire 80 additional cyber analysts and to increase the frequency of exercises that test its national-level response capability.

However, at this point, it is unclear whether these actions will help USCERT—or whatever organizational structure is ultimately charged with coordinating national cyber analysis and warning efforts—achieve the objectives set forth in policy. DHS faces a number of challenges that impede its ability to achieve its objectives, including fostering trusted relationships with critical infrastructure sectors, hiring and retaining skilled cyber analysts, ensuring that US-CERT warning products provide useful information in advance of attacks, enhancing predictive analysis, and ensuring that any changes brought about by HSPD 23 are marked by well-defined and transparent lines of authority and responsibility. We identified most of these challenges in our prior reviews and made broad recommendations to address them. DHS's actions to address these challenges have not been adequate. Because of this, addressing these challenges is as critical as ever to overcome the growing and formidable threats against our nation's critical cyber infrastructure. If these challenges are not addressed, US-CERT will not be able to provide an effective national cyber analysis and warning capability.

RECOMMENDATIONS FOR EXECUTIVE ACTION

We recommend that the Secretary of Homeland Security take four actions to fully establish a national cyber analysis and warning capability. Specifically, the Secretary should address deficiencies in each of the attributes identified for

- monitoring, including establish a comprehensive baseline understanding of the nation's critical information infrastructure and engage appropriate nonfederal stakeholders to support a national-level cyber monitoring capability;
- analysis, including expanding its capabilities to investigate incidents;
- warning, including ensuring consistent notifications that are targeted, actionable, and timely; and
- response, including ensuring that US-CERT provides assistance in the mitigation of and recovery from simultaneous severe incidents, including incidents of national significance.
- We also recommend that the Secretary address the challenges that impede DHS from fully implementing the key attributes, including the following 6 items:
- engaging appropriate stakeholders in federal and nonfederal entities to determine ways to develop closer working and more trusted relationships;
- expeditiously hiring sufficiently trained cyber analysts and developing strategies for hiring and retaining highly qualified cyber analysts;
- identifying and acquiring technological tools to strengthen cyber analytical capabilities and handling the steadily increasing workload;
- developing predictive analysis capabilities by defining terminology, methodologies, and indicators, and engaging appropriate stakeholders in other federal and nonfederal entities;

- filling key management positions and developing strategies for hiring and retaining those officials; and
- ensuring that there are distinct and transparent lines of authority and responsibility assigned to DHS organizations with cybersecurity roles and responsibilities, including the Office of Cybersecurity and Communications and the National Cybersecurity Center.

AGENCY COMMENTS AND OUR EVALUATION

In written comments on a draft of this chapter (see app. II), signed by the Director of DHS's GAO/OIG Liaison Office, the department concurred with 9 of our 10 recommendations. It also described actions planned and under way to implement the 9 recommendations. In particular, the department said that to fully establish a cyber analysis and warning capability, it plans to continue expansion of the Einstein intrusion detection system and increase US-CERT's staffing. In addition, to address the challenges that impede DHS from fully implementing key cyber analysis and warning attributes, the department stated that it plans to continue to build new relationships and grow existing ones with stakeholders. Further, to strengthen its analysis and warning capability and develop its predictive analysis capability, the department cited, among other things, its planned implementation of an upgraded version of Einstein.

DHS took exception to our last recommendation, stating that the department had developed a concept-of-operations document that clearly defined roles and responsibilities for the National Cybersecurity Center and NCSD. However, this concept-of-operations document is still in draft, and the department could not provide a date for when the document would be finalized and implemented.

DHS also commented on the report's description of US-CERT as "the center." Specifically, DHS was concerned that referring to US-CERT as the center might lead to confusion with the department's newly established National Cybersecurity Center. DHS requested that we remove references to US-CERT as the center. We agree with this comment and have incorporated it in the chapter where appropriate.

In addition to its written response, the department provided technical comments that have been incorporated in the chapter where appropriate.

We also incorporated technical comments provided by other entities involved in this review.

David A. Powner

Director,
Information Technology
Management Issues

Dr. Nabajyoti Barkakati
Acting Chief Technologist

APPENDIX I: OBJECTIVES, SCOPE, AND METHODOLOGY

Our objectives were to (1) identify key attributes of cyber analysis and warning capabilities, (2) compare these attributes with the United States Computer Emergency Readiness Team's (US-CERT) current analysis and warning capabilities to identify whether there are gaps, and (3) identify US-CERT's challenges to developing and implementing key attributes and a successful national cyber analysis and warning capability.

To identify key attributes of cyber analysis and warning capabilities, we identified entities based on our previous work related to cyber critical infrastructure protection, information security, and information sharing and analyzed relevant laws, strategies, and policies. In addition, we solicited suggestions from a variety of sources familiar with cyber analysis and warning organizations, including GAO's chief information technology officer and members of our Executive Council on Information Management and Technology, which is a group of executives with extensive experience in information technology management who advise us on major information management issues affecting federal agencies. On the basis of the entities identified, we selected those that were relevant and agreed to participate. We then gathered and analyzed policies, reports, and surveys; made site visits to observe the operation of cyber analysis and warning capabilities; conducted structured interviews; and received written responses to structured interview questions. These activities were performed, as appropriate, at the following entities:

- Department of Defense: Commander and Deputy Commander of the Joint Task Force—Global Network Operations and Director of the Defense Information Systems Agency; Commanding Officer, Navy Cyber Defense Operations Command; Chief Information Officer and Electronic

Data Service officials of the Navy's Global Network Operations Center. We also toured the Joint Task Force's Global Network Operations Center; the Navy's Cyber Defense Operation Command Center; and the Navy Marine Corps Intranet Network's Operations Center, Computer Incident Response Team Laboratory, Request Management Center, and Enterprise Global Networks Operations Center.
- Department of Energy: the Associate Chief Information Officer for Cyber Security for the Department of Energy and other relevant officials, and the Chief Information Officer of the National Nuclear Security Administration and other relevant officials.
- Department of Homeland Security: the Director of the National Cyber Security Division, the Acting Director of the National Cyber Security Division, and the Acting Director of US-CERT.
- National Institute of Standards and Technology: the Director of the Information Technology Laboratory and officials from the Information Technology Laboratory's Computer Security Division.
- Private sector: Carnegie Mellon University's CERT® Coordination Center, Internet Storm Center, LUMETA, Microsoft, MITRE, National Association of State Chief Information Officers, SANS Institute, SRI International, and Symantec.
- Information sharing and analysis centers representing the following sectors: financial services, information technology, states, surface transportation, and research and education.
- Federal agencies in the intelligence community.

On the basis of the evidence gathered and our observations regarding each entity's capabilities and operations, we determined the key common attributes of cyber analysis and warning capabilities. To verify the attributes we identified, we solicited comments from each entity regarding the attributes identified and incorporated the comments as appropriate.

To determine US-CERT's current national analysis and warning capabilities and compare them with the attributes identified to determine whether there were any gaps, we gathered and analyzed a variety of USCERT policies, procedures, and program plans to identify the organization's key activities related to cyber analysis and warning. We also observed US-CERT operations. In addition, we held interviews with key US-CERT officials, including the Director and Acting Director of the National Cyber Security Division, the Acting Director and Deputy Director of the US-CERT, and other relevant officials, to further clarify and confirm the key initiatives we identified through our analysis of the aforementioned documents. In addition, we interviewed the Director of

Intelligence for the Department of Homeland Security's Homeland Infrastructure Threat and Risk Analysis Center to determine that organization's interaction with US-CERT and its role regarding identifying cyber threats. We also interviewed the Deputy Director of the Department of Homeland Security's National Cybersecurity Center to obtain information about its concept-of-operations document. We then compared those activities to the key attributes of cyber analysis and warning capabilities in order to determine US-CERT's ability to provide cyber analysis and warning and identify any related gaps.

To identify US-CERT's challenges to developing and implementing the key attributes and a successful national cyber analysis and warning capability, we gathered and analyzed relevant documents, such as past GAO reports and studies by various cybersecurity-related entities, and interviewed key federal and nonfederal officials regarding the challenges associated with cyber analysis and warning. On the basis of the information received and our knowledge of the issues, we determined the major challenges to developing and implementing the key attributes and a successful national cyber analysis and warning capability.

We performed this performance audit between June 2007 and July 2008 in the Washington, D.C., metropolitan area; Atlanta, Georgia; Bloomington, Indiana; Pittsburgh, Pennsylvania; and Norfolk, Virginia; in accordance with generally accepted government auditing standards. Those standards require that we plan and perform the audit to obtain sufficient, appropriate evidence to provide a reasonable basis for our findings and conclusions based on our audit objectives. We believe that the evidence obtained provides a reasonable basis for our findings and conclusions based on our audit objectives.

Appendix II: Comments from the Department of Homeland Security

US GAO

2008 JUL -3 PM 2: 52

U.S. Department of Homeland Security
Washington, DC 20528

July 2, 2008

Mr. David Powner
Director
Information Technology Management Issues
United States Government Accountability Office
441 G Street, N.W.
Washington, DC 20001

Dear Mr. Powner:

> Re: Draft Report GAO-08-588, *Cyber Analysis and Warning: DHS Faces Challenges in Establishing a Comprehensive National Capability* (GAO Job Code 310851)

The Department of Homeland Security (DHS) appreciates the opportunity to review and comment on the subject draft report. We recognize that cyber threats are growing and are increasing in sophistication and accuracy. We also realize that as technology advances and our dependence on an interconnected cyberspace grows, the risks associated with cyber threats increase. The Department's National Protection and Programs Directorate (NPPD) National Cyber Security Division (NCSD) and its United States Computer Emergency Readiness Team (US-CERT)[1] are significantly changing and growing to address these cyber threats.

The federal government has undertaken a National Cybersecurity Initiative (NCI), which includes programs that strengthen US-CERT's capabilities for analyzing malicious activity, issuing warnings, and responding to incidents. With its newly expanded mission, budget and staff and a more customer-driven and outcome oriented culture, US-CERT will continue to increase its cyber analysis and warning capabilities. As US-CERT moves forward, the organization will work to address various recommendations set forth by GAO.

US-CERT is continually working to establish more effective outcome measures that will inform our program delivery and focus our resources on the most prevalent and highest risk issues. In addition to metrics analysis, US-CERT will continue to work with partners to determine how we can address the deficiencies identified by the GAO.

---

[1] Note: The Department requests that GAO use the acronym, "US-CERT," when referring to the United States Computer Emergency Readiness Team and remove any references to it as "the center." US-CERT is not classified or defined as a center by the Department or any other entity. The GAO's use of the term "the center" can be confusing because the report also refers to the National Cyber Security *Center* (NCSC), which is an organization separate from NCSD. The NCSC will not duplicate the roles and responsibilities of the participating organizations, such as US-CERT, but will support them and ensure coordination and shared cyber security situational awareness across these organizations.

www.dhs.gov

GAO Recommendation 1: *We recommend that the Secretary of Homeland Security–to fully establish a national cyber analysis and warning capability–specifically address deficiencies in monitoring, including establish a comprehensive baseline understanding of the nation's critical information infrastructure and engage appropriate nonfederal stakeholders to support a national-level cyber monitoring capability.*

Response: US-CERT concurs with this recommendation. Under the NCI, US-CERT is expanding its initial EINSTEIN program, referred to as EINSTEIN 1. The expanded program, referred to as EINSTEIN 2, is a 24x7 intrusion detection system that gathers network flow data from federal agencies and analyzes traffic patterns and behaviors. To improve US-CERT's capability to maintain situational awareness, all federal executive agencies, in accordance with the Office of Management and Budget (OMB) November 20, 2007, Memorandum M-08-05, Implementation of Trusted Internet Connection, will be required to use EINSTEIN 2. This expanded use of EINSTEIN 2 enables the US-CERT to gain increased situational awareness from all the federal executive agencies and fulfill its mandate to act as a central point for computer network security of the federal enterprise.

US-CERT does not directly monitor malicious activity involving nonfederal networks. However, NPPD and US-CERT actively reach out to private sector partners via various mechanisms to develop a baseline understanding of the nation's critical information infrastructure. NPPD Protective Security Advisors (PSAs) within the Office of Infrastructure Protection are located in field offices across the country and regularly conduct site visits to assess vulnerabilities, including cyber vulnerabilities, at Critical Infrastructure/Key Resource (CIKR) facilities. Further, NCSD co-chairs the Cross Sector Cyber Security Working Group under the National Infrastructure Protection Plan (NIPP) Framework, which includes representatives from all CIKR sectors and provides a monthly venue for engagement, collaboration and information sharing on cyber security issues.

A specific example of how the Department identifies specific vulnerabilities in the Nation's critical information infrastructure is the AURORA scenario, which involves the protective control systems used in the Nation's electric power grid. As soon as DHS identified this vulnerability, a Tiger Team of subject matter experts from government and industry was convened to determine the scope, potential consequences of this vulnerability, and to develop a better system for guiding private industry efforts to secure control systems. DHS is currently working with its government and industry partners to closely monitor this vulnerability, asses the risk it poses, and take appropriate proactive measures.

GAO Recommendation 2: *We recommend that the Secretary of Homeland Security–to fully establish a national cyber analysis and warning capability–specifically address deficiencies in analysis, including expanding its capabilities to investigate incidents.*

Response: We concur and are actively implementing improvements that will address the recommendation. Since January 2008, there has been an increase in funding of $115M in Fiscal Year 2008 for US-CERT. This funding includes salaries and benefits for 35 additional federal personnel and related costs, which will allow US-CERT to increase its cyber analysis and warning capabilities.

Much of the increased funding will be focused on developing and deploying EINSTEIN 2. EINSTEIN 2, like EINSTEIN 1, will continue to passively observe network traffic to and from participating federal executive agencies' networks. In addition, EINSTEIN 2 will alert when specific malicious network activity is detected and provide US-CERT with increased insight into the nature of that activity. Through EINSTEIN 2, US-CERT will be able to analyze malicious activity occurring across the federal IT networks resulting in improved computer network security situational awareness. This increase in situational awareness can then be shared with federal executive agencies in an effort to reduce and prevent computer network vulnerabilities.

EINSTEIN 2 adds to EINSTEIN 1 a network intrusion detection technology that will monitor for malicious activity in network traffic to and from participating federal executive agencies. EINSTEIN 2 will alert US-CERT when the system identifies malicious network traffic occurring in a federal executive agencies' network in response to specific predefined signatures. By scanning communications during transmission, EINSTEIN 2 identifies harmful communications that warrant analysis. A US-CERT analyst may then query that specific information in EINSTEIN 2 to analyze the potentially harmful network traffic identified by the alert.

EINSTEIN 2 is to augment -- not replace or reduce -- the current computer network security practices of participating federal executive agencies. Participating agencies will continue to operate their own intrusion detection and prevention systems, perform network monitoring, and use other information security technologies. EINSTEIN 2 enables US-CERT to correlate activity across the entire federal enterprise. With the enhanced correlation capability, US-CERT achieves increased situational awareness of federal executive agency computer networks which is required to perform the computer network security responsibilities assigned to DHS.

GAO Recommendation 3: *We recommend that the Secretary of Homeland Security–to fully establish a national cyber analysis and warning capability–specifically address deficiencies in warning, including ensuring consistent notifications that are targeted, actionable, and timely.*

Response: We concur with the recommendation. A key goal of US-CERT is to ensure that alerts—Critical Infrastructure Information Notices (CIINs) in particular—reach the appropriate stakeholders. US-CERT recognizes the importance of targeted information sharing and is working with NCSD's Outreach and Awareness Program and other cross sector working groups to increase awareness and communication channels.

The following communication channels are currently used for notification and activation in the event of a Cyber Incident:

- The National Cyber Alert System: This system provides an infrastructure, managed by US-CERT, for relaying timely and actionable computer security updates and warning information to all users.

- National Operations Center: This is the primary national-level hub for domestic incident management communications and operations.

- Homeland Security Information Network (HSIN) Critical Sector (CS): This communications network provides States and critical infrastructure owners and operators with real-time interactive connectivity to the National Operations Center (NOC) on a

Sensitive-but-Unclassified (SBU) level to all users. HSIN-CS is the NOC's primary suite of tools for information sharing, coordination, planning, mitigation, and response.

- US-CERT Portal: This secure collaboration tool enables private and public sectors to actively share information about cyber security vulnerabilities, exploits, and incidents in a trusted and secure environment among members.
- US-CERT Public Web Site: www.uscert.gov provides the primary means for US-CERT to convey information to the public at large. The site includes relevant information on cyber security issues, cyber activity, and vulnerability resources.
- Information Sharing and Analysis Centers (ISACs): Through secure websites and secure e-mail, information on infrastructure threats and vulnerabilities is provided to the members.

We do not agree with the report's repeated description of US-CERT's warnings and notifications as "not consistently actionable or timely (*i.e.*, providing the right information to the right person or group when needed)." We believe this statement inaccurately generalizes all US-CERT products. While US-CERT is charged with analyzing cyber threats and disseminating warning information, it relies on other stakeholders and entities such as ISACs, State, local, and tribal entities to review and maintain an accurate list of members who disseminate information to the correct personnel within their organization.[2]

GAO Recommendation 4: We recommend that the Secretary of Homeland Security—to fully establish a national cyber analysis and warning capability—specifically address deficiencies in response, including ensuring that US-CERT provides assistance in the mitigation and recovery from simultaneous severe incidents, including incidents of national significance.

Response: We concur and are actively implementing improvements for addressing the recommendation. While the Department is constantly enhancing its capabilities and currently increasing its budget and staffing, we do have recent examples of success in mitigating the effects of cyber incidents.

The GAO report mentioned the May 2007 denial-of-service cyber attack in Estonia; US-CERT successfully mitigated the effects of this attack. Bot-networks were flooding Estonia's IT systems with traffic, causing a denial of service for many of their government sites. US-CERT coordinated with its federal, international, and private sector partners to identify over 2,500 unique sources from 21 NATO countries participating in the attacking botnets on Estonia. The information was shared with military, intelligence, law enforcement, and US-CERT personnel from NATO member nations.

The GAO report also mentioned the Cyber Storm II exercise. The Cyber Storm II exercise, hosted by the Department of Homeland Security, helped participating organizations—public and private—prepare for, respond to, and mitigate cyber attacks that could affect their ability to

---

[2] With regard to targeted dissemination of US-CERT's vetted products [*e.g.*, Federal Information Notices (FINs), US-CERT CIINs issued via the Homeland Security Information Network – Critical Sectors (HSIN-CS) portal, and Situational Awareness Reports (SARs) US-CERT only vets the membership for the Government Forum of Incident Response and Security Teams (GFIRST)].

deliver critical services. This exercise is one of DHS's primary methods for enhancing crisis management and improving risk management across all participating organizations and highlights the interdependencies that exist between cyber and physical infrastructure. The exercise included elements of the private sector in the transportation, chemical, information technology, and communications sectors as well as federal agencies and departments and several international partners.

Also, EINSTEIN has proven successful in enhancing security within the federal government. Through the Department of Transportation's (DOT's) participation in the EINSTEIN program, US-CERT was able to quickly detect malicious activity and prevent it from infecting other government computers. In this case, a computer worm had infected an unsecured government computer in a U.S. Government agency. When the worm attempted to attack DOT's network, EINSTEIN detected the unusual traffic, and the subsequent US-CERT investigation uncovered the worm and worked with the affected departments and agencies to prevent its spread.

*GAO **Recommendation 5:*** *We recommend that the Secretary address the challenges that impede DHS from fully implementing the key attributes, including engaging appropriate stakeholders in federal and nonfederal entities to determine ways to develop closer working and more trusted relationships.*

Response: We concur and are actively implementing approaches for addressing the recommendation. Significant progress has been made in establishing or strengthening relationships with stakeholders, both internationally and domestically. The Department will continue to build new relationships and grow existing ones.

US-CERT coordinates information sharing and incident response activities with international partners to improve cyber incident response at the international level. US-CERT representatives participate in conferences to enhance international cyber coordination. US-CERT also meets individually with other countries' CERTs to discuss cyber incident mitigation and response strategies.

NCSD is committed to providing timely and actionable information on cyber incidents so that State cyber security responders can take appropriate action. Also, the information provided by State/local partners supplies important situational awareness for NCSD. There are channels in place that DHS uses to disseminate cyber information to State and local homeland security stakeholders.

- Government Forum of Incident Response and Security Teams (GFIRST): NCSD recently extended GFIRST membership to State and local governments. This is very significant as it links technical cyber experts in federal agencies with their counterparts in State/local governments and provides State/local governments access to tools and additional technical analysis. The GFIRST forum provides these technical experts with a collaborative space that will increase States' situational awareness of cyber incident response activity. US-CERT products and alerts are sent via the US-CERT-managed GFIRST portal.

- Multi-State Information Sharing and Analysis Center (MS-ISAC): The MS-ISAC membership is comprised of cyber officials from all States. NCSD provides funding to the MS-ISAC to assist with State/local coordination and information sharing on operational and other cyber security activities. NCSD provides a dedicated secure compartment within the US-CERT portal to enable collaboration among the State/local community and with NCSD/US-CERT. NCSD uses the Portal to both coordinate cyber awareness activities and initiatives, as well as disseminate critical cyber alerts and information. The MS-ISAC also maintains a distribution list of State and local points of contact, which allows NCSD to reach out to State/local decision makers regarding challenges, needs, and opportunities. In addition, NCSD participates in monthly calls with MS-ISAC membership and provides updates on Department activities and works with State/local representatives through established working groups that meet via monthly conference calls.

- Lessons Learned Information Sharing: NCSD has created a cyber security page on the LLIS.GOV site, which all homeland security personnel at the State and local level can access. NCSD populated this page with information regarding exercise after action reports, awareness materials, policies, plans, and other information on cyber security. States can post their best practices and materials here as well.

- Direct Contact: NCSD/US-CERT maintains positive relationships with numerous State points of contact and communicates/collaborates with them directly on a variety of topics.

GAO Recommendation 6: *We recommend that the Secretary address the challenges that impede DHS from fully implementing the key attributes, including expeditiously hiring sufficiently trained cyber analysts and developing strategies for hiring and retaining highly qualified cyber analysts.*

Response: We concur with the recommendation, and a strategy is already in place to address this need. DHS has recently entered into a contract to develop and implement a recruitment strategy to assist with cyber-related vacancies. NPPD has established an agreement with the Office of Personnel Management (OPM) to put a contracted human capital team in place to support the hiring requirement.

Vacancies are posted through a variety of internal and external mechanisms, including less traditional federal government venues, such as recruiting websites and various local newspapers. DHS and US-CERT participate in various career fairs and accepts referrals from other agencies and employees. Graduating students are also targeted through the Scholarship for Service program.

GAO Recommendation 7: *We recommend that the Secretary address the challenges that impede DHS from fully implementing the key attributes, including identifying and acquiring technological tools to strengthen cyber analytical capabilities and handling the steadily increasing workload.*

Response: We concur and are actively implementing approaches that address the recommendation. As described above, US-CERT is implementing an upgraded version of Einstein. Einstein 2 is an automated process for collecting, correlating, analyzing, and sharing computer security information across the Federal government so that Federal agencies are aware, in near real-time, of threats to infrastructure and can act swiftly to take corrective measures. It will incorporate network intrusion detection technology capable of alerting US-CERT to the presence of malicious or potentially harmful computer network activity in Federal executive agencies' network traffic.

In addition to implementing US-CERT's Einstein 2, DHS' Office of Science and Technology (S&T) and CS&C collaborate on cyber research and development (R&D) priorities to identify and develop technological tools to strengthen cyber analytical capabilities. Specifically, S&T created an Integrated Product Team (IPT) process to ensure proponents of R&D requirements, such as CS&C, are able to provide their requirements to S&T (i.e., existing capability shortfalls). A Research, Development, Test and Evaluation (RDT&E) program was established by S&T to address these requirements. CS&C developed a list of cyber security RDT&E requirements for the NCI which are in the process of being forwarded to S&T. These cyber related RDT&E requirements for critical infrastructures have been developed in a government-industry consensus process and are specified in the R&D portions of the Communications and IT Sector Specific Plans.

GAO Recommendation 8: *We recommend that the Secretary address the challenges that impede DHS from fully implementing the key attributes, including developing predictive analysis capabilities by defining terminology, methodologies, and indicators, and engaging appropriate stakeholders in other federal and nonfederal entities.*

Response: We concur and are actively implementing approaches that address the recommendation. EINSTEIN 2 uses anomaly-based detection methods to identify harmful or malicious computer network incidents. Anomaly-based detection, as defined in NIST Special Publication 800-94, is defined as "the process of comparing definitions of what activity is considered normal against observed events to identify significant deviations."

While an intrusion detection system uses a defined set of rules or filters that have been crafted to catch a specific, malicious event, the EINSTEIN 2 anomaly detection capability utilizes the network flow data and alerts to focus on the system's baseline of normal activity. As described above, behavior that varies from this standard is noted. Intrusion detection systems look for a misuse signature and anomaly detection looks for a strange event.

NCSD is also working with other Departmental and Interagency components to develop the strategic analysis of the Nation's critical cyber infrastructure, integrating all relevant and appropriate sources of information to support predictive analysis. NCSD is also seeking to engage stakeholders in other federal and nonfederal agencies to provide them with actionable information based on this predictive analysis.

GAO Recommendation 9: *We recommend that the Secretary address the challenges that impede DHS from fully implementing the key attributes, including filling key management positions and developing strategies for hiring and retaining those officials.*

Response: We concur with this recommendation. However, it is important to note that since the Exit Conference NCSD has filled several key management positions, including the positions of NCSD Director, US-CERT Director of Operations, and NCSD Chief of Staff. Further, DHS has recently entered into a contract to develop and implement a recruitment strategy to assist with cyber-related vacancies. NPPD has established an agreement with the Office of Personnel Management (OPM) to put a contracted human capital team in place to support the hiring requirement.

GAO Recommendation 10: *We recommend that the Secretary address the challenges that impede DHS from fully implementing the key attributes, including ensuring that there are distinct and transparent lines of authority and responsibility assigned to DHS organizations with cybersecurity roles and responsibilities, including the Office of Cyber Security and Communications and the National Cyber Security Center.*

Response: We do not concur with this recommendation. During the time period that GAO conducted their Cyber Analysis and Warning review, extensive interagency collaboration and coordination took place. This resulted in a NCSC Concept of Operations (CONOPS) with clearly defined roles and responsibilities for NCSC and NCSD. NCSC coordinates cyber security efforts and improves situational awareness and information sharing to support the entities defending government networks, such as US-CERT. US-CERT's ability to synthesize information and provide situational awareness will be enhanced through its work with the NCSC. The NCSC does not duplicate the roles and responsibilities of the participating organizations, such as US-CERT, but supports them in their mission and ensures coordination and shared cyber security situational awareness across these organizations.

Sincerely,

Jerald E. Levine
Director
Departmental GAO/OIG Liaison Office

REFERENCES

[1] Nonfederal entities include state and local governments, private sector entities, and academic institutions.

[2] Critical infrastructure is systems and assets, whether physical or virtual, so vital to the United States that their incapacity or destruction would have a debilitating impact on national security, national economic security, national public health or safety, or any combination of those matters. There are 18 critical infrastructure sectors: agriculture and food, banking and finance, chemical, commercial facilities, communications, critical manufacturing, dams, defense industrial base, emergency services, energy, government facilities, information technology, national monuments and icons, nuclear reactors, materials and waste, postal and shipping, public health and health care, transportation systems, and water.

[3] Statement of the Director of National Intelligence before the Senate Select Committee on Intelligence, *Annual Threat Assessment of the Director of*

National Intelligence for the Senate Select Committee on Intelligence (Feb. 5, 2008).

[4] Robert McMillan, "Seagate Ships Virus-Laden Hard Drives," InfoWorld (San Francisco, California: InfoWorld Media Group, Nov. 12, 2007), http://www.infoworld.com/ article/07/11/12/Seagate-ships-virus-laden-hard-drives_1.html (accessed Apr. 9, 2008).

[5] GAO, *Critical Infrastructure Protection: Department of Homeland Security Faces Challenges in Fulfilling Cybersecurity Responsibilities*, GAO-05-434 (Washington, D.C.: May 26, 2005).

[6] GAO, *Critical Infrastructure Protection: Multiple Efforts to Secure Control Systems Are Under Way, but Challenges Remain*, GAO-08-119T (Washington, D.C.: Oct. 17, 2007).

[7] GAO-08-119T.

[8] Computer Emergency Response Team of Estonia, "Malicious Cyber Attacks Against Estonia Come from Abroad," April 29, 2007, and Remarks by Homeland Security Secretary Michael Chertoff to the 2008 RSA Conference, April 8, 2008.

[9] Office of the Secretary of Defense, *Annual Report to Congress: Military Power of the People's Republic of China 2008*.

[10] Homeland Security Act of 2002, Pub. L. 107-296 (Nov. 25, 2002).

[11] The White House, *The National Strategy to Secure Cyberspace* (Washington, D.C.: February 2003).

[12] The White House, *Homeland Security Presidential Directive 7, Critical Infrastructure Identification, Prioritization, and Protection* (Washington, D.C.: Dec. 17, 2003).

[13] GAO-05-434.

[14] GAO, *Critical Infrastructure Protection: Significant Challenges in Developing National Capabilities*, GAO-01-323 (Washington, D.C.: Apr. 25, 2001).

[15] Department of Homeland Security, *National Response Framework* (Washington, D.C.: January 2008).

[16] The White House, *National Security Presidential Directive 54/Homeland Security Presidential Directive 23* (Washington, D.C.: Jan. 8, 2008).

[17] Nonfederal entities include state and local governments, private sector entities, and individuals.

[18] The CERT Coordination Center is a center of Internet security expertise at the Software Engineering Institute, a federally funded research and development center operated by the Carnegie Mellon University. CERT Coordination Center is registered in the U.S. Patent and Trademark Office by Carnegie Mellon University.

[19] ISACs are to facilitate the private sector's participation in critical infrastructure protection efforts by serving as mechanisms for gathering and analyzing information and sharing it among the critical infrastructure sectors and between the private sector and government. ISACs have been established for many sectors, including financial services, electricity, information technology, research and education, the states, and telecommunications.

[20] According to the National Institute of Standards and Technology, the National Vulnerability Database is the U.S. government repository of standards-based vulnerability management data. These data enable automation of vulnerability management, security measurement, and compliance (e.g., to meet the requirements of the Federal Information Security Management Act). This database includes databases of security checklists, security-related software flaws, misconfigurations, product names, and impact metrics.

[21] According to MITRE, the Common Vulnerabilities and Exposures (CVE®) list is a dictionary of common names (i.e., CVE Identifiers) for publicly known information security vulnerabilities. CVE's common identifiers make it easier to share data across separate information security databases and tools, and provide a baseline for evaluating the coverage of an organization's security tools.

[22] According to NIST, the Common Vulnerability Scoring System (CVSS) is an open framework for communicating the characteristics and impacts of IT vulnerabilities. Specifically, CVSS provides a standard measurement system for industries, organizations, and governments that need accurate and consistent vulnerability impact scores.

[23] According to MITRE, Open Vulnerability and Assessment Language (OVAL™) is an international information security community standard to promote open and publicly available security content, and to standardize the transfer of this information across the entire spectrum of security tools and services.

[24] The SANS Internet Storm Center (ISC) is an example of a cooperative cyber analysis and warning center. The ISC provides free analysis and warning services for those who monitor the Web site. Participation is voluntary. In addition, the SANS Institute sponsors intrusion detection software that acts as a monitoring sensor for data collection from which threat information and data trends can be analyzed.

[25] Computer forensics is the practice of gathering, retaining, and analyzing computer-related data for investigative purposes in a manner that maintains the integrity of the data.

[26] A honeypot is an intentionally underprotected computer host that is designed to collect data on suspicious activity. It generally has no authorized users other

than its administrators. A sandbox is an isolated computer host used by analysts to let them observe cyber threats in order to gather data about how a specific threat might act. It is used to observe threats without endangering a live network and proprietary data.

[27] NIST, *Computer Security Incident Handling Guide: Recommendations of the National Institute of Standards and Technology,* Special Publication 800-6 1 Revision 1 (Gaithersburg, Maryland: March 2008). This guide was issued to assist organizations in establishing computer security incident response capabilities and in handling incidents efficiently and effectively.
[28] NIST Special Pub. 800-61 Rev. 1.
[29] NIST Special Pub. 800-61, Rev. 1.
[30] Cyber Storm is a biennial national-level exercise to test the ability of federal and nonfederal stakeholders, including federal, state, and local agencies; private sector entities; and foreign governments, to respond to major cyber attacks. The last exercise, referred to as Cyber Storm II, was held in March 2008.
[31] GAO, *Critical Infrastructure Protection: Multiple Efforts to Secure Control Systems Are Under Way, but Challenges Remain,* GAO-07-1036 (Washington, D.C.: Sept. 10, 2007).
[32] GAO-01-323.
[33] GAO-05-434.
[34] GAO-05-207.
[35] GAO-05-434.
[36] GAO-05-434.

In: Cybersecurity, Cyberanalysis and Warning ISBN: 978-1-60692-658-1
Editors: K. T. Norwood et al © 2009 Nova Science Publishers, Inc.

Chapter 2

CRITICAL INFRASTRUCTURE PROTECTION. DHS NEEDS TO BETTER ADDRESS ITS CYBERSECURITY RESPONSIBILITIES[*]

David Powner

Mr. Chairman and Members of the Subcommittee:

Thank you for the opportunity to join in today's hearing to discuss efforts in protecting our nation's critical infrastructures from cybersecurity threats. The recent computer-based, or cyber, attacks against nation-states and others demonstrate the potentially devastating impact these pose to systems and the operations and critical infrastructures that they support.[1] They also highlight the need to be vigilant against individuals and groups with malicious intent, such as criminals, terrorists, and nation-states perpetuating these attacks.

Today, I will discuss the Department of Homeland Security's (DHS) progress in fulfilling its responsibilities to protect systems that support critical infrastructures— a practice referred to as cyber critical infrastructure protection or cyber CIP—as well as its progress in addressing our related recommendations. Due to concerns about DHS's efforts to fully implement its CIP responsibilities as well as known security risks to critical infrastructure systems, we added cyber CIP as part of our federal information technology systems security high-risk area in 2003 and have continued to report on its status since that time.[2]

---

[*] Excerpted from GAO Report GAO-08-1157T, dated September 16, 2008.

As requested, my testimony will summarize our key reports—two of which are being released today at this hearing—and their associated recommendations aimed at securing our nation's cyber critical infrastructure. Specifically, these reports and recommendations focus on (1) providing cyber analysis and warning capabilities, (2) being effectively organized to plan for and respond to disruptions on .converged voice and data networks, (3) conducting and coordinating cyber attack exercises, (4) developing cyber-related sector-specific critical infrastructure plans, (5) securing control systems—computer-based systems that monitor and control sensitive processes and physical functions, and (6) coordinating public/private planning for Internet recovery from a major disruption.

In preparing for this testimony, we relied on our previous reports on department efforts to fulfilling its cyber CIP responsibilities. These reports contain detailed overviews of the scope and methodology we used. We also obtained and analyzed information about the implementation status of our recommendations. We conducted our work, in support of this testimony, from August 2008 through September 2008, in the Washington, D.C. area. The work on which this testimony is based was performed in accordance with generally accepted government auditing standards.

RESULTS IN BRIEF

Since 2005, we have reported that DHS has yet to fully satisfy its cybersecurity responsibilities. These reports included nearly 30 recommendations on key areas essential for DHS to address in order to fully implement its cybersecurity responsibilities. Examples of what GAO reported and recommended are as follows:

- *Cyber analysis and warning*—In a report being released today, we determined[3] that DHS's United States Computer Emergency Readiness Team (US-CERT) did not fully address 15 key cyber analysis and warning attributes related to (1) monitoring network activity to detect anomalies, (2) analyzing information and investigating anomalies to determine whether they are threats, (3) warning appropriate officials with timely and actionable threat and mitigation information, and (4) responding to the threat. For example, US-CERT provided warnings by developing and distributing a wide array of notifications; however, these notifications were not consistently actionable or timely. As a result, we recommended that the department address shortfalls associated with the 15 attributes in order to fully establish a national cyber analysis and warning capability. DHS agreed in large part with our recommendations.

- *Cyber exercises*—In another report[4] being issued today, we concluded that since conducting a major cyber attack exercise, called Cyber Storm, DHS demonstrated progress in addressing eight lessons it learned from these efforts. However, its actions to address the lessons had not been fully implemented. Specifically, while it had completed 42 of the 66 activities identified, the department identified 16 activities as ongoing and 7 as planned for the future. Consequently, we recommended that it schedule and complete all of the corrective activities identified so as to strengthen coordination between both public and private sector participants in response to significant cyber incidents. DHS concurred with our
- *Control systems*—In a September 2007 report and October 2007 testimony,[5] we identified that DHS was sponsoring multiple control systems security initiatives, including efforts to (1) improve control systems cybersecurity using vulnerability evaluation and response tools and (2) build relationships with control systems vendors and infrastructure asset owners. However, DHS had not established a strategy to coordinate the various control systems activities across federal agencies and the private sector, and it did not effectively share information on control system vulnerabilities with the public and private sectors. Accordingly, we recommended that DHS develop a strategy to guide efforts for securing control systems and establish a rapid and secure process for sharing sensitive control system vulnerability information to improve federal government efforts to secure control systems governing critical infrastructure. DHS officials took our recommendations under advisement and more recently have begun developing a strategy, which is still a work in process. In addition, while DHS has begun developing a process to share sensitive information, it has not provided any evidence that the process has been implemented or that it is an effective information sharing mechanism.

BACKGROUND

The same speed and accessibility that create the enormous benefits of the computer age can, if not properly controlled, allow individuals and organizations to inexpensively eavesdrop on or interfere with computer operations from remote locations for mischievous or malicious purposes, including fraud or sabotage. In recent years, the sophistication and effectiveness of cyberattacks have steadily advanced.

Government officials are increasingly concerned about attacks from individuals and groups with malicious intent, such as criminals, terrorists, and nation-states. As we reported[6] in June 2007, cybercrime has significant economic impacts and threatens U.S. national security interests. Various studies and experts estimate the direct economic impact from cybercrime to be in the billions of dollars annually. In addition, there is continued concern about the threat that our adversaries, including nation-states and terrorists, pose to our national security. For example, intelligence officials have stated that nation-states and terrorists could conduct a coordinated cyber attack to seriously disrupt electric power distribution, air traffic control, and financial sectors. In May 2007, Estonia was the reported target of a denial-of-service cyber attack with national consequences. The coordinated attack created mass outages of its government and commercial Web sites.[7]

To address threats posed against the nation's computer-reliant infrastructures, federal law and policy establishes DHS as the focal point for cyber CIP. For example, within DHS, the Assistant Secretary of Cyber Security and Communications is responsible for being the focal point for national cyber CIP efforts. Under the Assistant Secretary is NCSD which interacts on a day-to-day basis with federal and nonfederal agencies and organizations (e.g., state and local governments, private-sector companies) regarding, among other things, cyber-related analysis, warning, information sharing, major incident response, and national-level recovery efforts. Consequently, DHS has multiple cybersecurity-related roles and responsibilities. In May 2005, we identified, and reported on, 13 key cybersecurity responsibilities called for in law and policy.[8] These responsibilities are described in appendix I.

Since then, we have performed detailed work and made recommendations on DHS's progress in fulfilling specific aspects of the responsibilities, as discussed in more detail later in this statement.

In addition to DHS efforts to fulfill its cybersecurity responsibilities, the President in January 2008 issued HSPD 23—also referred to as National Security Presidential Directive 54 and the President's "Cyber Initiative"—to improve DHS and the other federal agencies' cybersecurity efforts, including protecting against intrusion attempts and better anticipating future threats.[9] While the directive has not been made public, DHS officials stated that the initiative includes steps to enhance cyber analysis related efforts, such as requiring federal agencies to implement a centralized network monitoring tool and reduce the number of connections to the Internet.

DHS NEEDS TO ADDRESS SEVERAL KEY AREAS ASSOCIATED WITH ITS CYBERSECURITY RESPONSIBILITIES

Over the last several years, we have reported that DHS has yet to comprehensively satisfy its key cybersecurity responsibilities. These reports included about 30 recommendations that we summarized into the following key areas that are essential for DHS to address in order to fully implement its cybersecurity responsibilities.

Table 1. Key Cybersecurity Areas Reviewed by GAO

1. Bolstering cyber analysis and warning capabilities.
2. Reducing organizational inefficiencies.
3. Completing actions identified during cyber exercises.
4. Developing sector-specific plans that fully address all of the cyber-related criteria.
5. Improving cybersecurity of infrastructure control systems.
6. Strengthening DHS's ability to help recover from Internet disruptions.

Bolstering Cyber Analysis and Warning Capabilities

In July 2008, we identified [10] that cyber analysis and warning capabilities included (1) monitoring network activity to detect anomalies, (2) analyzing information and investigating anomalies to determine whether they are threats, (3) warning appropriate officials with timely and actionable threat and mitigation information, and (4) responding to the threat. These four capabilities are comprised of 15 key attributes, which are detailed in appendix II.

We concluded that while US-CERT demonstrated aspects of each of the key attributes, it did not fully incorporate all of them. For example, as part of its monitoring, US-CERT obtained information from numerous external information sources; however, it had not established a baseline of our nation's critical network assets and operations. In addition, while it investigated if identified anomalies constitute actual cyber threats or attacks as part of its analysis, it did not integrate its work into predictive analyses of broader implications or potential future attacks, nor does it have the analytical or technical resources to analyze multiple, simultaneous cyber incidents. The organization also provided warnings by developing and distributing a wide array of attack and other notifications; however, these notifications were not consistently actionable or timely—providing the right information to the right persons or groups as early as possible to give them time to take appropriate action. Further, while it responded to a limited number of affected entities in their efforts to contain and mitigate an attack, recover from damages, and remediate vulnerabilities, the organization did not possess the resources to handle multiple events across the nation.

We also concluded that without the key attributes, US-CERT did not have the full complement of cyber analysis and warning capabilities essential to effectively perform its national mission. As a result, we made 10 recommendations to the department to address shortfalls associated with the 15 attributes in order to fully establish a national cyber analysis and warning capability. DHS concurred with 9 of our 10 recommendations.

Reducing Organizational Inefficiencies

In June 2008, we reported[11] on the status of DHS's efforts to establish an integrated operations center that it agreed to adopt per recommendations from a DHS-commissioned expert task force. The two operations centers that were to be integrated were within the department's National Communication System and National Cyber Security Division. We determined that DHS had taken the first of three steps towards integrating the operations centers—called the National Coordination Center Watch and US-CERT—it uses to plan for and monitor voice and data network disruptions. While DHS completed the first integration step by locating the two centers in adjacent space, it had yet to implement the remaining two steps. Specifically, although called for in the task force's recommendations, the department had not organizationally merged the two centers or involved key private sector critical infrastructure officials in the planning, monitoring, and other activities of the proposed joint operations center. In addition, the department lacked a strategic plan and related guidance that provides overall direction in this area and has not developed specific tasks and milestones for achieving the two remaining integration steps.

We concluded that until the two centers were fully integrated, DHS was at risk of being unable to efficiently plan for and respond to disruptions to communications infrastructure and the data and applications that travel on this infrastructure, increasing the probability that communications will be unavailable or limited in times of need. As a result, we recommended that the department complete its strategic plan and define tasks and milestones for completing remaining integration steps so that we are better prepared to provide an integrated response to disruptions to the communications infrastructure. DHS concurred with our first recommendation and stated that it would address the second recommendation as part of finalizing its strategic plan.

DHS has recently made organizational changes to bolster its cybersecurity focus. For example, in response to the President's January 2008 Cyber Initiative, the department established a National Cybersecurity Center to ensure coordination among cyber-related efforts across the federal government. DHS placed the center at a higher organizational level than the Assistant Secretary of Cyber Security and Communications. As we previously reported,[12] this placement raises questions about, and may in fact, diminish the Assistant Secretary's authority as the focal point for the federal government's cyber CIP efforts. It also raises similar questions about NCSD's role as the primary federal cyber analysis and warning organization.

Completing Corrective Actions Identified During a Cyber Exercise

In September 2008, we reported[13] on a 2006 major DHS-coordinated cyber attack exercise, called Cyber Storm, that included large scale simulations of multiple concurrent attacks involving the federal government, states, foreign governments, and private industry. We determined that DHS had identified eight lessons learned from this exercise, such as the need to improve interagency coordination groups and the exercise program. We also concluded that while DHS had demonstrated progress in addressing the lessons learned, more needed to be done. Specifically, while the department completed 42 of the 66 activities identified to address the lessons learned, it identified 16 activities as ongoing and 7 as planned for the future.[14] In addition, DHS provided no timetable for the completion dates of the ongoing activities. We noted that until DHS scheduled and completed its remaining activities, it was at risk of conducting subsequent exercises that repeated the lessons learned during the first exercise. Consequently, we recommended that DHS schedule and complete the identified corrective activities so that its cyber exercises can help both public and private sector participants coordinate their responses to significant cyber incidents. DHS agreed with the recommendation.

Developing Sector-Specific Plans that Fully Address All of the Cyber-Related Criteria

In 2007, we reported and testified[15] on the cybersecurity aspects of CIP plans for 17 critical infrastructure sectors, referred to as sector- specific plans. Specifically, we found that none of the plans fully addressed the 30 key cybersecurity-related criteria described in DHS guidance. We also determined that while several sectors' plans fully addressed many of the criteria, others were less comprehensive. In addition to the variations in the extent to which the plans covered aspects of cybersecurity, there was also variance among the plans in the extent to which certain criteria were addressed. For example, fewer than half of the plans fully addressed describing (1) a process to identify potential consequences of cyber attack or (2) any incentives used to encourage voluntary performance of risk assessments. We noted that without complete and comprehensive plans, stakeholders within the infrastructure sectors may not adequately identify, prioritize, and protect their critical assets. Consequently, we recommended[16] that DHS request that the lead federal agencies, referred to as sector-specific agencies, that are responsible for the development of CIP plans for their sectors fully address all cyber-related criteria by September 2008 so that stakeholders within the infrastructure sectors will effectively identify, prioritize, and protect the cyber aspects of their CIP efforts. The updated plans are due this month.

Improving Cybersecurity of Infrastructure Control Systems

In a September 2007 report and October 2007 testimony,[17] we identified that federal agencies had initiated efforts to improve the security of critical infrastructure control systems—computer-based systems that monitor and control sensitive processes and physical functions. For example, DHS was sponsoring multiple control systems security initiatives, including efforts to (1) improve control systems cybersecurity using vulnerability evaluation and response tools and (2) build relationships with control systems vendors and infrastructure asset owners. However, the department had not established a strategy to coordinate the various control systems activities across federal agencies and the private sector. Further, it lacked processes needed to address specific weaknesses in sharing information on control system vulnerabilities. We concluded that until public and private sector security efforts are coordinated by an overarching strategy and specific information sharing shortfalls are addressed, there was an increased risk that multiple organizations would conduct duplicative work and miss opportunities to fulfill their critical missions.

Consequently, we recommended[18] that DHS develop a strategy to guide efforts for securing control systems and establish a rapid and secure process for sharing sensitive control system vulnerability information to improve federal government efforts to secure control systems governing critical infrastructure. In response, DHS officials took our recommendations under advisement and more recently have begun developing a Federal Coordinating Strategy to Secure Control Systems, which is still a work in process. In addition, while DHS began developing a process to share sensitive information; it has not provided any evidence that the process has been implemented or that it is an effective information sharing mechanism.

Strengthening DHS's Ability to Help Recovery from Internet Disruptions

We reported and later testified[19] in 2006 that the department had begun a variety of initiatives to fulfill its responsibility for developing an integrated public/private plan for Internet recovery. However, we determined that these efforts were not comprehensive or complete. As such, we recommended that DHS implement nine actions to improve the department's ability to facilitate public/private efforts to recover the Internet in case of a major disruption.

In October 2007, we testified[20] that the department had made progress in implementing our recommendations; however, seven of the nine have not been completed. For example, it revised key plans in coordination with private industry infrastructure stakeholders, coordinated various Internet recovery-related activities, and addressed key challenges to Internet recovery planning. However, it had not, among other things, finalized recovery plans and defined the interdependencies among DHS's various working groups and initiatives. In other words, it has not completed an integrated private/public plan for Internet recovery. As a result, we concluded that the nation lacked direction from the department on how to respond in such a contingency. We also noted that these incomplete efforts indicated DHS and the nation were not fully prepared to respond to a major Internet disruption.

In summary, DHS has developed and implemented capabilities to satisfy aspects of key cybersecurity responsibilities. However, it still needs to take further action to fulfill all of these responsibilities. In particular, it needs to fully address the key areas identified in our recent reports. Specifically, it will have to bolster cyber analysis and warning capabilities, address organizational inefficiencies by integrating voice and data operations centers, enhance cyber exercises by completing the identified activities associated with the lessons learned, ensure that cyber-related sector-specific critical infrastructure plans are completed, improve efforts to address the cybersecurity of infrastructure control systems by completing a comprehensive strategy and ensuring adequate mechanisms for sharing sensitive information, and strengthen its ability to help recover from Internet disruptions by finalizing recovery plans and defining interdependencies. Until these steps are taken, our nation's computer-reliant critical infrastructure remains at unnecessary risk of significant cyber incidents.

Mr. Chairman, this concludes my statement. I would be happy to answer any questions that you or members of the subcommittee may have at this time.

If you have any questions on matters discussed in this testimony, please contact me at (202) 512-9286, or by e-mail at pownerd@gao.gov. Other key contributors to this testimony include Camille Chaires, Michael Gilmore, Rebecca LaPaze, Kush Malhotra, and Gary Mountjoy.

APPENDIX I: DHS'S KEY CYBERSECURITY RESPONSIBILITIES

Responsibilities	Description of responsibilities
Develop a national plan for CIP that includes cybersecurity	Developing a comprehensive national plan for securing the key resources and critical infrastructure of the United States, including information technology and telecommunications systems (including satellites) and the physical and technological assets that support such systems. This plan is to outline national strategies, activities, and milestones for protecting critical infrastructures.
Develop partnerships and coordinate with other federal agencies, state and local governments, and the private sector	Fostering and developing public/private partnerships with and among other federal agencies, state and local governments, the private sector, and others. DHS is to serve as the "focal point for the security of cyberspace."
Improve and enhance public/private information sharing involving cyber attacks, threats, and vulnerabilities	Improving and enhancing information sharing with and among other federal agencies, state and local governments, the private sector, and others through improved partnerships and collaboration, including encouraging information sharing and analysis mechanisms. DHS is to improve sharing of information on cyber attacks, threats, and vulnerabilities.
Provide and coordinate incident response and recovery planning efforts	Providing crisis management in response to threats to or attacks on critical information systems. This entails coordinating efforts for incident response, recovery planning, exercising cybersecurity continuity plans for federal systems, planning for recovery of Internet functions, and assisting infrastructure stakeholders with cyber-related emergency recovery plans.
Identify and assess cyber threats and vulnerabilities	Leading efforts by the public and private sector to conduct a national cyber threat assessment, to conduct or facilitate vulnerability assessments of sectors, and to identify cross-sector interdependencies.

Responsibilities	Description of responsibilities
Support efforts to reduce cyber threats and vulnerabilities	Leading and supporting efforts by the public and private sector to reduce threats and vulnerabilities. Threat reduction involves working with the law enforcement community to investigate and prosecute cyberspace threats. Vulnerability reduction involves identifying and remediating vulnerabilities in existing software and systems.
Promote and support research and development efforts to strengthen cyberspace security	Collaborating and coordinating with members of academia, industry, and government to optimize cybersecurity-related research and development efforts to reduce vulnerabilities through the adoption of more secure technologies.
Foster training and certification	Improving cybersecurity-related education, training, and certification opportunities.
Enhance federal, state, and local government cybersecurity	Partnering with federal, state, and local governments in efforts to strengthen the cybersecurity of the nation's critical information infrastructure to assist in the deterrence, prevention, preemption of, and response to terrorist attacks against the United States.
Strengthen international cyberspace security	Working in conjunction with other federal agencies, international organizations, and industry in efforts to promote strengthened cybersecurity on a global basis.
Integrate cybersecurity with national security	Coordinating and integrating applicable national preparedness goals with its National Infrastructure Protection Plan.

Source: GAO analysis of the Homeland Security Act of 2002, the Homeland Security Presidential Directive-7, and the National Strategy to Secure Cyberspace.

APPENDIX II: KEY ATTRIBUTES OF CYBER ANALYSIS AND WARNING CAPABILITIES

Capability	Attribute
Monitoring	• Establish a baseline understanding of network assets and normal network traffic volume and flow • Assess risks to network assets • Obtain internal information on network operations via technical tools and user reports • Obtain external information on threats, vulnerabilities, and incidents through various relationships, alerts, and other sources • Detect anomalous activities
Analysis	• Verify that an anomaly is an incident (threat of attack or actual attack) • Investigate the incident to identify the type of cyber attack, estimate impact, and collect evidence • Identify possible actions to mitigate the impact of the incident • Integrate results into predictive analysis of broader implications or potential future attack
Warning	• Develop attack and other notifications that are targeted and actionable • Provide notifications in a timely manner • Distribute notifications using appropriate communications methods

(Continued).

Capability	Attribute
Response	• Contain and mitigate the incident • Recover from damages and remediate vulnerabilities • Evaluate actions and incorporate lessons learned

Source: GAO analysis.

REFERENCES

[1] Critical infrastructure is systems and assets, whether physical or virtual, so vital to the United States that their incapacity or destruction would have a debilitating impact on national security, national economic security, national public health or safety, or any combination of those matters. There are 18 critical infrastructure sectors: agriculture and food, banking and finance, chemical, commercial facilities, communications, critical manufacturing, dams, defense industrial base, emergency services, energy, government facilities, information technology, national monuments and icons, nuclear reactors, materials and waste, postal and shipping, public health and health care, transportation systems, and water.

[2] For our most recent high risk report, see GAO, *High-Risk Series: An Update*, GAO-07-310 (Washington, D.C.: January 2007)

[3] GAO, Cyber Analysis and Warning: DHS Faces Challenges in Establishing a Comprehensive National Capability, GAO-08-588 (Washington, D.C.: July 31, 2008).

[4] GAO, Critical Infrastructure Protection: DHS Needs To Fully Address Lessons Learned from Its First Cyber Storm Exercise, GAO-08-825 (Washington, D.C.: Sept. 9, 2008).

[5] GAO, Critical Infrastructure Protection: Multiple Efforts to Secure Control Systems Are Under Way, but Challenges Remain, GAO-07-1036 (Washington, D.C.: Sept. 10, 2007) and Critical Infrastructure Protection: Multiple Efforts to Secure Control Systems Are Under Way, but Challenges Remain, GAO-08-119T (Washington, D.C.: Oct. 17, 2007)

[6] GAO, *Cybercrime: Public and Private Entities Face Challenges in Addressing Cyber Threats*, GAO-07-705 (Washington, D.C.: June 22, 2007).

[7] Computer Emergency Response Team of Estonia, "Malicious Cyber Attacks Against Estonia Come from Abroad," April 29, 2007, and Remarks by Homeland

Security Secretary Michael Chertoff to the 2008 RSA Conference, April 8, 2008.
[8] GAO, *Critical Infrastructure Protection: Department of Homeland Security Faces Challenges in Fulfilling Cybersecurity Responsibilities*, GAO-05-434 (Washington, D.C.: May 26, 2005); *Critical Infrastructure Protection: Challenges in Addressing Cybersecurity*, GAO-05-827T (Washington, D.C.: July 19, 2005); and *Critical Infrastructure Protection: DHS Leadership Needed to Enhance Cybersecurity*. GAO-06-1087T (Washington, D.C.: Sept. 13, 2006).
[9] The White House, National Security Presidential Directive 54/Homeland Security Presidential Directive 23 (Washington, D.C.: Jan. 8, 2008).
[10] GAO-08-588.
[11] GAO, *Critical Infrastructure Protection: Further Efforts Needed to Integrate Planning for and Response to Disruption on Converged Voice and Data Networks*, GAO-08-607 (Washington, D.C.: June 26, 2008).
[12] GAO-08-588.
[13] GAO-08-825.
[14] DHS reported that one other activity had been completed, but the department was unable to provide evidence demonstrating its completion.
[15] GAO, *Critical Infrastructure Protection: Sector-Specific Plans' Coverage of Key Cyber Security Elements Varies*, GAO-08-64T (Washington D.C.; October 31, 2007); and *Critical Infrastructure Protection: Sector-Specific Plans' Coverage of Key Cyber Security Elements Varies*, GAO-08-113 (Washington D.C.; Oct. 31, 2007).
[16] GAO-08-113.
[17] GAO-07-1036 and GAO-08-119T.
[18] GAO-07-1036.
[19] GAO, *Internet Infrastructure: Challenges in Developing a Public/Private Recovery Plan*, GAO-06-863T (Washington, D.C.: July 28, 2006); and *Internet Infrastructure: DHS Faces Challenges in Developing a Joint Public/Private Recovery Plan*, GAO-06-672 (Washington, D.C.: June 16, 2006).
[20] GAO, *Internet Infrastructure: Challenges in Developing a Public/Private Recovery Plan*, GAO-08-212T (Washington, D.C.: Oct. 23, 2007)

In: Cybersecurity, Cyberanalysis and Warning
Editors: K. T. Norwood et al.
ISBN: 978-1-60692-658-1
© 2009 Nova Science Publishers, Inc.

Chapter 3

CRITICAL INFRASTRUCTURE PROTECTION. DHS NEEDS TO FULLY ADDRESS LESSONS LEARNED FROM ITS FIRST CYBER STORM EXERCISE[*]

U.S Government Accountability Office

ABBREVIATIONS

DHS	Department of Homeland Security
ISAC	Information Sharing and Analysis Center
NCRCG	National Cyber Response Coordination Group
NCSD	National Cyber Security Division
US-CERT	United States Computer Emergency Readiness Team

September 9, 2008
The Honorable
Bennie G. Thompson
Chairman

---

[*] Excerpted from GAO Report GAO-08-825, dated September 2008.

Committee on Homeland Security
House of Representatives

The Honorable
James R. Langevin
Chairman

Subcommittee on Emerging Threats, Cybersecurity,
and Science and Technology
Committee on Homeland Security
House of Representatives

Since the early 1990s, increasing computer interconnectivity—most notably growth in the use of the Internet—has revolutionized the way that our government, our nation, and much of the world communicate and conduct business. While the benefits of this technology have been enormous, this widespread interconnectivity poses significant risks to the government's and our nation's computer systems and, more important, to the critical operations and infrastructures they support.

Federal policies establish the Department of Homeland Security (DHS) as the focal point for the security of cyberspace—including analysis, warning, information sharing, vulnerability reduction, mitigation, and recovery efforts for public and private critical infrastructure systems.[1] To accomplish this mission, DHS is to work with federal agencies, state and local governments, and the private sector. Federal policy also recognizes the importance of building public/private partnerships because the private sector owns a large percentage of the nation's critical infrastructure— including banking and financial institutions, telecommunications networks, and energy production and transmission facilities.

As part of DHS's cybersecurity responsibilities, the agency is required to coordinate cyber attack simulation exercises to strengthen public and private incident response capabilities. One major exercise program, called Cyber Storm, is a large-scale simulation of multiple concurrent cyber attacks involving the federal government, states, foreign governments, and private industry. To date, DHS has conducted Cyber Storm exercises in 2006 and 2008, and it is currently planning a third for 2010. Because of your interest in these exercises, we agreed to (1) identify the lessons that DHS learned from the first Cyber Storm exercise, (2) assess DHS's efforts to address the lessons learned from this exercise, and (3) identify key participants' views of their experiences during the second Cyber Storm exercise.

To address these objectives, we reviewed relevant DHS documents, including the Cyber Storm I Exercise Report, a list of planned post-Cyber Storm activities, and artifacts showing actions taken to address activities. We attended the second Cyber Storm exercise, held in Washington, D.C., in March 2008. We also interviewed DHS officials responsible for planning the exercises as well as participants in the Cyber Storm exercises, including officials representing three federal agencies, three private industry sectors, and one representing state governments. In addition, this work builds on a body of work we have done over the last several years on the cyber aspects of critical infrastructure protection.[2]

We performed our work from January to September 2008 in accordance with generally accepted government auditing standards. Those standards require that we plan and perform the audit to obtain sufficient, appropriate evidence to provide a reasonable basis for our findings and conclusions based on our audit objectives. We believe that the evidence obtained provides a reasonable basis for our findings and conclusions based on our audit objectives. Additional details on our objectives, scope, and methodology are provided in appendix I.

RESULTS IN BRIEF

As a result of its first Cyber Storm exercise, in February 2006, DHS identified eight lessons that had significant impact across sectors, agencies, and exercise participants. These lessons involved improving (1) the interagency coordination groups; (2) contingency planning, risk assessment, and roles and responsibilities; (3) integration of incidents across infrastructures; (4) access to information; (5) coordination of response activities; (6) strategic communications and public relations; (7) processes, tools, and technology; and (8) the exercise program.

While DHS has demonstrated progress in addressing the lessons it learned from its first Cyber Storm exercise, more remains to be done to fully address the lessons. In the months following its first exercise, DHS identified 66 activities that address one or more of the lessons, including hosting meetings with key cyber response officials from foreign, federal, and state governments and private industry; refining operating procedures; and obtaining new tools and technologies to support incident response operations. Since that time, DHS has completed 42 of these activities.[3] However, key activities have not yet been completed. DHS identified 16 activities as ongoing and 7 as planned for the future. In addition, while DHS identified completion dates for its planned activities, it has not identified completion dates associated with activities that are reported as ongoing. For example, DHS reports that it has work under way to issue guidance to information sharing and analysis centers on public communications related to cybersecurity, but has not established a milestone for completing this activity. Until DHS schedules and completes its remaining activities, the agency risks conducting subsequent exercises that repeat the lessons learned during the first exercise.

Commenting on their experiences during the second Cyber Storm exercise in March 2008, participants observed both progress and continuing challenges in building a comprehensive national cyber response capability. Their observations addressed several key areas, including the value and scope of the exercise, roles and responsibilities, public relations, communications, the exercise infrastructure, and the handling of classified information. For example, many participants reported that their organizations found value in the exercise because it led them to update their contact lists and improve their response capabilities. Other participants, however, reported the need for clarifying the role of the law enforcement community during a cyber incident and for improving policies governing the handling of classified information so that key information can be shared. Many of the challenges noted during Cyber Storm II were similar to ones identified during the first exercise.

We are making a recommendation to the Secretary of Homeland Security to direct the Assistant Secretary for Cybersecurity and Communications to oversee the completion of corrective activities resulting from Cyber Storm I, many of which were reiterated during Cyber Storm II. DHS provided written comments on a draft of this chapter (see app. IV). In its comments, DHS concurred with our recommendation and reported that the department is working to complete applicable activities identified during the first Cyber Storm exercise. DHS officials also provided technical comments, which we have incorporated as appropriate.

BACKGROUND

Critical infrastructures are physical or virtual systems and assets so vital to the nation that their incapacitation or destruction would have a debilitating impact on national security, national economic security, national public health or safety, or any combination of these matters. These systems and assets—such as the electric power grid, chemical plants, and water treatment facilities—are essential to the operations of the economy and the government. Recent terrorist attacks and threats have underscored the need to protect our nation's critical infrastructures. If vulnerabilities in these infrastructures are exploited, they could be disrupted or disabled, leading to physical damage, economic losses, and even loss of life.

The Federal Government Plays a Critical Role in Helping Secure Critical Infrastructures

Federal law and policies call for critical infrastructure protection activities to enhance the physical and cybersecurity of both public and private infrastructures that are essential to national security, economic well-being, and national public health and safety.[4] Federal policies identify 18 critical infrastructure sectors and designate certain federal agencies as lead points of contact for each (see table 1). Further, they assign these agencies responsibility for infrastructure protection activities in their assigned sectors and for coordination with other relevant federal agencies, state and local governments, and the private sector. In addition, federal policies establish DHS as the focal point for the security of cyberspace—including analysis, warning, information sharing, vulnerability reduction, mitigation, and recovery efforts for public and private critical infrastructure systems.

Table 1. Critical Infrastructure Sectors and Their Lead Agencies

Sector	Description	Lead agency
Agriculture and food	Provides for the fundamental need for food. The infrastructure includes supply chains for feed and crop production, processing, and retail sales.	Department of Agriculture, Department of Health and Human Services, Food and Drug Administration a
Banking and finance	Provides the financial infrastructure of the nation. This sector consists of commercial banks, insurance companies, mutual funds, governmentsponsored enterprises, pension funds, and other financial institutions that carry out transactions, including clearing and settlement.	Department of the Treasury
Chemical	Transforms natural raw materials into commonly used products benefiting society's health, safety, and productivity. The chemical industry produces more than 70,000 products that are essential to automobiles, pharmaceuticals, food supply, electronics, water treatment, health, construction, and other necessities.	Department of Homeland Security

Table 1. (Continued).

Sector	Description	Lead agency
Commercial facilities	Includes prominent commercial centers, office buildings, sports stadiums, theme parks, and other sites where large numbers of people congregate to pursue business activities, conduct personal commercial transactions, or enjoy recreational pastimes.	Department of Homeland Security
Commercial nuclear reactors, materials, and waste	Includes 104 commercial nuclear reactors; research and test nuclear reactors; nuclear materials; and the transportation, storage, and disposal of nuclear materials and waste.	Department of Homeland Security
Dams	Comprises approximately 80,000 dam facilities, including larger and nationally symbolic dams that are major components of other critical infrastructures that provide electricity and water.	Department of Homeland Security
Defense industrial base	Supplies the military with the means to protect the nation by producing weapons, aircraft, and ships and providing essential services, including information technology and supply and maintenance.	Department of Defense
Drinking water and water treatment systems	Sanitizes the water supply through about 170,000 public water systems. These systems depend on reservoirs, dams, wells, treatment facilities, pumping stations, and transmission lines.	Environmental Protection Agency
Emergency services	Saves lives and property from accidents and disasters. This sector includes fire, rescue, emergency medical services, and law enforcement organizations.	Department of Homeland Security
Energy	Provides the electric power used by all sectors and the refining, storage, and distribution of oil and gas. This sector is divided into electricity and oil and natural gas.	Department of Energy
Government facilities	Includes the buildings owned and leased by the federal government for use by federal entities.	Department of Homeland Security
Information technology	Produces hardware, software, and services that enable other sectors to function.	Department of Homeland Security

Sector	Description	Lead agency
National monuments and icons	Includes key assets that are symbolically identified with traditional American values and institutions or U.S. political and economic power.	Department of the Interior
Manufacturing	Includes key critical manufacturing operations based on highly integrated and interdependent supply chains. This sector provides metal, machinery, electrical equipment, appliances, components, and transportation equipment.	Department of Homeland Security
Postal and shipping	Delivers private and commercial letters, packages, and bulk assets. The United States Postal Service and other carriers provide the services of this sector.	Department of Homeland Security
Public health and health care	Mitigates the risk of disasters and attacks and also provides recovery assistance if an attack occurs. This sector consists of health departments, clinics, and hospitals.	Department of Health and Human Services
Telecommunications	Provides wired, wireless, and satellite communications to meet the needs of businesses and governments.	Department of Homeland Security
Transportation systems	Enables movement of people and assets that are vital to our economy, mobility, and security, using aviation, ships, rail, pipelines, highways, trucks, buses, and mass transit.	Department of Homeland Security

Source: GAO analysis of The National Infrastructure Protection Plan, Homeland Security Presidential Directive 7, and the National Strategy for Homeland Security.

[a] The Department of Agriculture is responsible for food (meat, poultry, and eggs) and agriculture; and the Department of Health and Human Services, Food and Drug Administration, is responsible for food other than meat, poultry, and egg products.

DHS Organization Is the Focal Point for National Cybersecurity Efforts

In June 2003, DHS created the National Cyber Security Division (NCSD), to serve as a national focal point for addressing cybersecurity issues and to coordinate the implementation of the National Strategy to Secure Cyberspace (the Cyberspace

Strategy). Its mission is to secure cyberspace and America's cyber assets in cooperation with public, private, and international entities. NCSD reports to the Assistant Secretary for Cybersecurity and Communications.

A key component of NCSD, the U.S. Computer Emergency Readiness Team (US-CERT), is an operational organization responsible for analyzing and addressing cyber threats and vulnerabilities and disseminating cyber threat warning information. In the event of an Internet disruption, USCERT facilitates coordination of recovery activities with the network and security operations centers of owners and operators of the Internet and with government incident response teams. We recently reported on USCERT's challenges in establishing a comprehensive national cyber analysis and warning capability.[5]

NCSD also cochairs the National Cyber Response Coordination Group (NCRCG), which includes officials from the agencies that have a responsibility for cybersecurity as well as the lead agencies for different critical infrastructure sectors.[6] This group is the principal federal interagency mechanism for coordinating the response to and recovery from significant national cyber incidents. In the event of a major incident, NCRCG is responsible for providing subject matter expertise, recommendations, and strategic policy support to the Secretary of Homeland Security.

In addition, DHS recently announced that it is establishing a new National Cyber Security Center that is to report directly to the Secretary of Homeland Security. According to the Assistant Secretary for Cybersecurity and Communications, this center will be responsible for ensuring coordination among the cyber-related efforts across the federal government and improving situational awareness and information sharing to support the entities defending government networks, including USCERT.

DHS Is Responsible for Conducting and Coordinating Cyber Exercises to Improve National Preparedness, Response, and Recovery Capabilities

Federal policies call for DHS to establish a national exercise program to improve the nation's ability to prevent, prepare for, respond to, and recover from terrorist attacks, major disasters, and other emergencies.[7] More specifically, the Cyberspace Strategy calls for DHS to conduct cybersecurity exercises to evaluate the impact of cyber attacks on governmentwide processes and to explore the use of such exercises to test coordination of public and private incident management, response, and recovery capabilities. Further, in its National Infrastructure Protection

Plan, DHS states that it will conduct national cyber exercises to improve cyber preparedness, response, coordination, and recovery capabilities. [8]

To address its cyber exercise responsibilities, DHS works with other federal agencies, state and city governments, regional coalitions, and international partners. DHS's role can range from providing cyber scenarios or expertise to local or regional exercises, cosponsoring exercises, or conducting its own large-scale cyber attack simulations (called Cyber Storm exercises). See table 2 for examples of recent and planned cyber exercises.

Table 2. Recent and Planned Cyber Exercises

Date	Exercise name	Description	Participant(s)
September 2004	Blue Cascades II	Cosponsored by DHS and organized by members of the Pacific Northwest Economic Region. This exercise tested regional capabilities to deal with threats, interdependencies, and cascading impacts by simulating a series of attacks that disrupted infrastructures and organizations, including critical telecommunications and electricity assets.	Federal, state, and local governments and private industry
October 2004	Purple Crescent II	Sponsored by the Gulf Coast Regional Partnership for Infrastructure Security and funded by DHS. The exercise was designed to raise awareness of infrastructure interdependencies and identify how to improve regional preparedness by simulating cyber attacks on regional infrastructures as well as government and private organizations during an approaching hurricane.	Federal, state, and local governments; academic institutions; and private industry
April 2005	Top Officials-3	Sponsored by DHS, this exercise was to evaluate decision making by federal, state, and local governments by simulating terrorist threats and attacks involving chemicals, biological agents, and explosives.	Federal, state, local, and foreign governments and private industry

Table 2. (Continued).

Date	Exercise name	Description	Participant(s)
April 2005	Multi-State Information Sharing and Analysis Center's Tabletop Exercise	Cosponsored by DHS and the Multi-State Information Sharing and Analysis Center during the center's annual meeting. This tabletop exercise was designed to offer an opportunity for the state information technology participants to discuss their state policies and procedures and to prepare for the Cyber Storm I exercise.	State governments
February 2006	Cyber Storm I	Sponsored by DHS, Cyber Storm I was the first large-scale national cyber exercise to improve incident response and coordination capabilities by simulating multiple cyber incidents affecting the energy, information technology, telecommunications, and transportation critical infrastructure sectors.	Federal, state, and foreign governments and private industry
March 2006	Blue Cascades III	Cosponsored by DHS and organized by members of the Pacific Northwest Economic Region. This exercise was designed to focus on efforts to recover and restore services by simulating the impact of a major earthquake in the area.	Federal, state, local, and foreign governments and private industry
October 2006	Delaware Cyber Security Tabletop Exercise	Sponsored by the state of Delaware, with assistance from DHS. This exercise was designed to discuss the technical implications of a pandemic disaster scenario.	State government
December 2006	Cyber Tempest	Cosponsored by DHS and the New York State Office of Cyber Security and Critical Infrastructure Coordination. This exercise was designed to focus on regional stakeholders' procedures for response and coordination during emergencies.	State government

Date	Exercise name	Description	Participant(s)
April 2007	Multi-State Information Sharing and Analysis Center's Tabletop Exercise	Cosponsored by DHS and the Multi-State Information Sharing and Analysis Center during the center's annual meeting. This exercise was designed to offer an opportunity for the state information technology participants to discuss their state policies and procedures and to prepare for the Cyber Storm II exercise.	State government
September 2007	ChicagoFIRST Exercise	Cosponsored by DHS and ChicagoFIRST, a nonprofit organization representing financial institutions. This exercise was designed to offer the city government an opportunity to collaborate with greater Chicago regional stakeholders.	Local/regional government
October 2007	Top Officials-4	Sponsored by DHS. This exercise was designed to test federal, state, territorial, and local response capabilities by simulating coordinated attacks using a radiological dispersal device.	Federal, state, local, and foreign governments and private industry
October 2007	Illinois Cyber Tabletop Exercise	Sponsored by the state of Illinois, with assistance from DHS. This exercise was designed to provide participants with an opportunity to discuss a cyber scenario affecting multiple state critical infrastructures, resulting in cascading effects across the state.	State government
October 2007	Delaware Cyber Security Tabletop Exercise	Sponsored by the state of Delaware, with assistance from DHS. The exercise was designed to discuss the increasing threat of financial and identify thefts with stakeholders.	State government
March 2008	Cyber Storm II	Sponsored by DHS, this exercise was to improve national incident response and coordination capabilities by simulating physical and cyber attacks against the transportation, information technology, and chemical critical infrastructure sectors.	Federal, state, and foreign governments and private industry

Table 2. (Continued).

Date	Exercise name	Description	Participant(s)
May 2008	Massachusetts Cyber Exercise	Cosponsored by DHS and the state of Massachusetts. This exercise was to examine processes, procedures, and the operational architecture of system operators, law enforcement officials, local/state government, and several private sector partners in response to specific cyber attack scenarios.	State and local governments
September 2008	Chicago FIRST Exercise	Cosponsored by DHS and ChicagoFIRST. This exercise is planned to focus on the financial sector.	Private industry

Source: GAO analysis of DHS data.

DHS's Cyber Storm Exercises

DHS's Cyber Storm exercises are intended to examine national preparedness, response, coordination, and recovery efforts when faced with a large-scale cyber incident. Participants include federal and state agencies, private industry representatives, and selected foreign governments. DHS conducted Cyber Storm exercises in 2006 and 2008, and is planning to conduct a third exercise in 2010.

In February 2006, DHS conducted Cyber Storm I at a cost of about $3.7 million. The exercise simulated a large-scale attack affecting the energy and transportation infrastructures, using the telecommunications infrastructure as a medium for the attack. Participants included eight federal departments and three agencies, three states, and four foreign countries. The exercise also involved representatives from the private sector—including 11 information technology companies, 7 electric companies, 1 banking and finance company, and 2 airlines—and over 100 public and private agencies, associations, and corporations. DHS officials conducted the exercise primarily on a separate network to minimize the impact on "real world" information systems. The objectives of Cyber Storm I were to

- exercise interagency coordination by convening NCRCG and the Interagency Incident Management Group, a multi-agency team of federal

executives responsible for providing strategic advice during nationally significant incidents;[9]
- exercise intergovernmental and intragovernmental coordination and incident response;
- identify policies and issues that hinder or support cybersecurity requirements;
- identify public/private interface communications and thresholds of coordination to improve cyber incident response and recovery, as well as identify critical information sharing paths and mechanisms;
- identify, improve, and promote public and private sector interaction in processes and procedures for communicating appropriate information to key stakeholders and the public;
- identify cyber and physical infrastructure interdependencies with real world economic and political impact;
- raise awareness of the economic and national security impacts associated with a significant cyber incident; and
- highlight available tools and technologies with analytical cyber incident response and recovery capabilities.

In March 2008, DHS conducted its second broad-scale exercise, called Cyber Storm II. The exercise cost about $6.4 million, and simulated a large-scale cyber attack affecting the communications, information technology, chemical, and transportation infrastructures. According to DHS, the exercise involved 18 federal agencies, 9 states, 10 information sharing and analysis centers, 5 foreign countries, and over 40 industry representatives from the private sector. The objectives of Cyber Storm II were to

- examine the capabilities of participating organizations to prepare for, protect from, and respond to the effects of cyber attacks;
- exercise senior leadership decision making and interagency coordination of incident responses in accordance with national-level policies and procedures;
- validate information sharing relationships and communication paths for the collection and dissemination of cyber incident situational awareness, response, and recovery information; and
- examine the means and processes to share sensitive and classified information across standard boundaries in safe and secure ways without compromising proprietary or national security interests.

DHS plans to issue a report on what it learned from Cyber Storm II by the end of 2008.

DHS IDENTIFIED EIGHT LESSONS DURING CYBER STORM I

While Cyber Storm I participants reported that the exercise was valuable in that it helped them establish and improve interagency and public/private response relationships, DHS also identified eight lessons during the Cyber Storm I exercise that affected all participating sectors and agencies. These lessons involved improving (1) the interagency coordination groups; (2) contingency planning, risk assessment, and roles and responsibilities; (3) integration of incidents across infrastructures; (4) access to information; (5) coordination of response activities; (6) strategic communications and public relations; (7) processes, tools, and technology; and (8) the exercise program.

Interagency Coordination Groups

DHS reported that during the exercise, the two key interagency coordination groups—NCRCG and the Interagency Incident Management Group—were convened appropriately and that they worked well together. For example, the two groups coordinated to develop a refined awareness of the attack situation and to assess effects on the nation's critical infrastructure. However, the agency found that a broader understanding of how these groups operate would improve coordination, both within the government and with the private sector. Specifically, participants reported that

- greater collaboration could be achieved if the private sector was allowed interaction with NCRCG during major incidents,
- additional work was needed to determine how to effectively elevate the alert levels in response to cyber attacks or threats,
- NCRCG did not have enough technical experts on staff to fully leverage the large volume of incident information,
- communication procedures were needed to deliver key technical messages at a layman's level to organizations' public affairs groups in a timely manner, and
- an established information sharing process between NCRCG and allied nations would facilitate communication and help ensure a more effective response.

Contingency Planning, Risk Assessment, and Roles and Responsibilities

DHS found that formal contingency planning, risk assessment, and the definition of roles and responsibilities across the entire cyber community must continue to be solidified. It reported that in cases where procedures were clear and fully understood by participants, incident responses were timely and well coordinated. However, in cases where there were no previously established relationships and procedures for coordinating responses and assessing risks were not clear, participants had difficulty determining which organizations and people to contact. In addition, DHS found that contingency planning for backup or resilient communications was critical. The agency noted that during the exercise many participants relied heavily on communications systems that could be vulnerable to attack or failure.

Integration of Incidents Across Infrastructures

According to DHS, the integration of multiple incidents across multiple infrastructures and between the public and private sectors remained a challenge. DHS reported that the cyber incident response community was generally effective in addressing single threats or attacks and, to some extent, in addressing multiple threats and attacks when these incidents were treated as individual and discrete events. However, participants were challenged when attempting to develop an integrated situational awareness and to understand the impact of multiple attacks across sectors. As the organization responsible for analyzing cyber threats and disseminating warnings, US-CERT had a lead role in forming an integrated situational awareness. However, during the exercise, US-CERT was inundated with information and questions from both the public and the private sectors. The US-CERT team found that the volume of information limited its ability to simultaneously provide situational awareness coordination and conduct technical analyses. Participants reported that a prioritization scheme is needed in order to rapidly assess cyber incidents, their sources, and their applicability to the broad-scale attack. In addition, DHS noted that there needs to be greater clarification of US-CERT's roles, responsibilities, and procedures.

Access to Information

While DHS reported that a continuous flow of information created a common framework for responding to the incidents, the majority of exercise participants reported difficulty in identifying accurate and up-to-date sources of information. For example, during the exercise, participants received multiple alerts on a single issue, which created confusion and made it more difficult to establish a single coordinated response. Participants observed that establishing a single point of contact for information would allow a common framework for responses, and noted that US-CERT is the correct agency to disseminate time sensitive and critical information to the appropriate organizations. In addition, while US-CERT provided significant information in the form of alerts and technical bulletins, participants stated that US-CERT's capabilities to post information in a timely, secure, and accurate manner needed to be further explored.

Coordination of Response Activities

DHS found that coordinating responses became more challenging as the number of cyber events increased, thus highlighting the importance of cooperation and communication. For example, during the exercise, participants noted the overwhelming effects that multiple, simultaneous, and coordinated attacks had on their response activities, which proved that the ability to accurately fuse information is crucial for responding appropriately to simultaneous attacks. Participants reported that clarifying roles and responsibilities across government, as well as the expectations between public and private sectors, is needed to coordinate preventive measures and responses to disruptions.

Strategic Communications and Public Relations

DHS reported that public messaging must be an integral part of plans for responding to a cyber incident in order to provide critical information to the response community and to empower the public to take appropriate actions. Exercise participants stated that publicly released information could undermine consumer confidence, and noted the importance of aligning both public and private sector public relations plans in order to have a coordinated approach during a crisis. In addition, DHS found that federal responses to cyber incidents must include public affairs teams to ensure that press releases and accurate situation updates are provided to partner organizations and media outlets.

DHS reported that improved processes, tools, and training for analyzing and prioritizing the physical, economic, and national security impacts of cyber attack scenarios would enhance the quality, speed, and coordination of response. In particular, participants reported that exchanging and sharing classified information was a challenge and suggested that processes be developed to downgrade classified information so that it could be shared throughout the response community.

The Exercise Program

DHS reported that recurring exercises would strengthen participants' awareness of organizational cyber incident response, roles, policies, and procedures. Participants observed that ongoing training, discussions, and exercises are needed to build relationships among organizations and to strengthen the coordination of responses to cyber incidents. In addition, several participants in Cyber Storm I recommended the execution of smaller, more routine exercises.

DHS HAS DEMONSTRATED PROGRESS IN ADDRESSING LESSONS FROM ITS FIRST CYBER STORM EXERCISE, BUT MORE REMAINS TO BE DONE

While DHS has demonstrated progress in addressing the lessons it learned from its first Cyber Storm exercise, more remains to be done to fully address the lessons. Federal policy requires that DHS develop and maintain a system to collect, analyze, and disseminate lessons learned, best practices, and information from exercises, training events, and other sources.[10] In addition, DHS's homeland security exercise program guidance requires that, following an exercise, planners must identify a list of corrective actions and track their implementation.[11]

DHS has begun to fulfill these requirements. Specifically, DHS documented the lessons it learned during the first Cyber Storm exercise and identified 66 activities that address one or more of the lessons. These activities included hosting meetings with key cyber response officials from foreign, federal, and state governments and private industry; refining the procedures under which these entities operate; and participating in smaller cyber exercises to test these refined procedures (see app. II for a list of activities).

In addition, DHS has made progress in completing its planned activities, but more remains to be done. Of the 66 activities intended to address the lessons, 42 activities have been completed. These completed activities range from clarified procedures to improved technology for emergency responders, and they should improve communications and response activities during a significant cyber incident. DHS reported that another activity had been completed, but was unable to provide evidence demonstrating its completion. However, key activities needed to improve coordination and response during a significant cyber incident have not yet been completed. The remaining 23 activities include 16 activities that are ongoing and 7 activities that are planned for the future. While DHS has identified completion dates for its planned activities, it has not identified completion dates associated with activities that are reported as ongoing. For example, DHS reported that it has work under way to issue guidance to information sharing and analysis centers on public communications related to cybersecurity, but has not identified a milestone for completing this activity. Table 3 provides the number of activities in each of these categories.

Table 3. Summary of Status of Activities

Status of DHS activities	Number of activities
Reported and validated as completed	42
Reported as completed, but not validated due to insufficient evidence	1
Reported as ongoing	16
Reported as planned for the future	7
Total	66

Focusing on each of the eight lessons, DHS has completed selected activities within each lesson, but has more to do. The department's progress on each of the lessons learned during the first Cyber Storm exercise is discussed below. In reviewing this progress, it is important to note that because many of DHS's activities are intended to address more than one lesson, the sum of the activities supporting all eight lessons is higher than the net number of activities. Specifically, DHS listed 121 activities to address lessons 1 through 8, but 55 of these repeat a prior activity. A complete list of the activities supporting each lesson and their status are provided in appendix III.

- *Interagency coordination groups*—DHS identified 32 activities to address the need for improving the interagency coordination groups. Of these, 24 activities have been completed and 8 are ongoing or planned for the future. DHS completed activities such as researching and procuring situation awareness visualization and communication tools and conducting a tabletop exercise among NCRCG, the Homeland Security Operations Center, the Crisis Action Team, and US-CERT. Activities that still remain to be completed include establishing secure communications with all

international partners and working with leadership to frame possible changes in rules for raising alert levels.
- *Contingency planning, risk assessment, and roles and responsibilities*—DHS identified 15 activities to address the need for improved contingency planning, risk assessment, and roles and responsibilities. Of these, 8 activities had been completed and 7 are ongoing or planned for the future. DHS completed activities such asresearching secure cell phone capability for NCRCG members and procuring satellite phones. Activities that still remain to be completed include coordinating standard operating procedures and concepts of operations with several information sharing and analysis centers and establishing a continuity-of-operations plan.
- *Integration of incidents across infrastructures*—DHS identified 16 activities to address the need for improved integration of incidents across infrastructures. Of these, 9 have been completed and 7 are ongoing or planned for the future. Completed activities include meeting with international participants to share capabilities and establish working relationships and researching alternatives to the Emergency Notification System. Activities that still remain to be completed include filling open spots at US-CERT to better address its mission and coordinating standard operating procedures with US-CERT and the information technology and communications information sharing and analysis centers.
- *Access to information*—DHS identified 15 activities to address the need for improved access to information. Of these, 8 activities have been completed and 7 are ongoing or planned for the future. DHS completed developing a contact list of key public and private sector subject matter experts and meeting with international participants to share capabilities and establish working relationships. Activities that still remain to be completed include identifying and organizing a private sector counterpart for NCRCG and establishing processes, procedures, and physical means to communicate securely with counterparts.
- *Coordination of response activities*—DHS identified 15 activities to address the need for improved coordination of response activities. Of these, 11 have been completed and 4 are ongoing or planned for the future. DHS completed activities such as significantly revising the NCRCG's standard operating procedures and refining situation report development and communication within those procedures. Activities that still remain to be completed include developing policies for handling classified information and educating the law enforcement community on the role and function of NCRCG.

- *Strategic communications and public relations plan*—DHS identified 5 activities to address the lesson that public messaging must be an integral part of contingency planning and incident response. Of these, 1 activity has been completed and 4 are ongoing or planned for the future. DHS completed efforts to establish a mechanism for communicating real world implications of cyber incidents to DHS Public Affairs and the Public Affairs Working Group. Activities that still remain to be completed include issuing guidance to information sharing and analysis centers on a set of policies for cybersecurity-related public communications and developing public affairs messaging coordination between public and private information technology organizations for normal and emergency operations.
- *Processes, tools, and technology*—DHS identified 12 activities to address the need for improved processes, tools, and technology. Of these, 8 activities have been completed and 4 are ongoing or planned for the future. Completed activities include developing a comprehensive set of cyber scenarios to support the exercises and clarifying interfaces and expectations at every level of NCRCG engagement. Activities that still remain to be completed include requesting that all federal computer emergency response teams obtain secure communications and developing policies for handling classified information.
- *Exercise program*—DHS identified 11 activities to address the need for improvements to the exercise program. Of these, 9 activities have been completed and 2 are ongoing or planned for the future. Completed activities include participating in a tabletop exercise and a full-scale exercise, and improving the communications infrastructure for the exercise. DHS has not yet completed activities including implementing a relational database consistent with industry standards in order to allow better correlation, analysis, and communication of incidents.

Until DHS schedules and completes its planned corrective activities, the agency risks wasting resources on subsequent exercises that repeat the lessons it learned in its first exercise.

CYBER STORM II PARTICIPANTS OBSERVED PROGRESS AND CONTINUED CHALLENGES IN EXERCISING THE NATIONAL CYBER RESPONSE CAPABILITY

Commenting on their experiences during Cyber Storm II, participants observed both progress and continued challenges in building a comprehensive national cyber response capability. Their observations addressed several key areas, including the value and scope of the exercise, roles and responsibilities, public relations, communications, the exercise infrastructure, and the handling of classified information.

Exercise value and scope—The participants we met with reported that their organization found value in participating in the exercise. For example, one agency official stated that the exercises were invaluable because they allowed the agency to update call lists and to practice how it would respond to cyber events. In addition, a participant stated that the exercise had a positive outcome for his organization and that the real benefit of the exercise was in sharing information.

However, participants agreed that smaller, more frequent exercises would be helpful in planning for cyber incidents. One agency official stated that the "doomsday" scenarios made it difficult to test agencies' responses to less dramatic cyber incidents. Another agency official reported that the sheer number of e-mail alerts received during the exercise was difficult to handle. Another participant suggested that DHS conduct exercises focusing on different infrastructure sectors during every quarterly meeting of NCRCG.

Roles and responsibilities—Cyber Storm II participants reported having a much better understanding of the various organizations' roles and whom to contact within those organizations during a cyber incident. For example, a participant noted that NCRCG has had time to stabilize over the 2 years since the first Cyber Storm exercise.

However, participants also reported that there is room for improvement in defining the roles and responsibilities of both NCRCG and the law enforcement community. Specifically, selected Information Sharing and Analysis Center (ISAC) members reported that there is still confusion in the private sector on NCRCG's role during a cyber incident. ISAC officials stated that it was unclear to the private sector what NCRCG is responsible for, what it means when the group is activated, and what this activation means to the private sector. In addition, Cyber Storm II participants reported the need for further clarification of the roles and responsibilities of the law enforcement community during a cyber incident. Specifically, law enforcement participants noted that other exercise participants may not have been properly reporting incidents to the law enforcement community, even though most scenarios involved criminal violations. They stated that not being appropriately involved in the exercise scenarios made it difficult to fully test investigative and legal processes.

Public relations—While participants generally agreed that media relations went well during the exercise, they also identified the need for further improvements. To address prior concerns, DHS included a public relations specialist in the NCRCG membership to help develop messages for NCRCG and other organizations involved in the exercise, and provided a technical specialist to the department's public affairs office to ensure cyber issues were described accurately. However, a private sector participant commented that there appeared to be minimal alignment of communications and public relations plans between the public and private sectors during the exercise.

Communications—Participants also reported a need for further improvement in communication between participants during the exercise. For example, a private sector participant cited a breakdown in communication where participants were not aware that the US-CERT alert level had been raised. Another participant reported that US-CERT did not resolve conflicting data before issuing information—even after this individual's ISAC contacted US-CERT. In another instance, a private sector participant reported not knowing how to contact US-CERT during the exercise. Another participant reported that there were instances where private sector players were sharing information with DHS, but the information appeared never to have made it to the decision makers.

Exercise infrastructure—Participants generally agreed that improvements to the exercise's infrastructure could be made. For example, several participants reported that DHS was not able to use an encrypted communications system it developed for the exercise because the technology failed. However, DHS reported that the technology did not fail, but rather that it turned off the technology because of security concerns. Participants also reported issues with receiving e-mails of the exercises, downloading the exercise directory, and accessing the exercise's Web page. Another participant stated that his organization did not have time to run some of the exercise scenarios due to technical issues it encountered during the exercise.

Classified information handling—Participants stated that there is a continuing challenge in accessing sensitive information on cyber threats and incidents, and that policies dealing with classified information need to be improved. For example, one private sector participant stated that it is not clear how information gets classified or what information is available to the private sector. An agency official stated that it has been a challenge to pull unclassified information out of classified information systems in order to share it. Other participants stated that they would like to see additional effort expended on sharing unclassified information on the government's public response portal—the Government Forum of Incident Response and Security Teams portal—which is available to federal agencies and to a limited number of local agencies and organizations. Participants noted that the portal is too open for truly secure communication but not open enough to share information between public and private sectors.

Many of the challenges that participants noted during Cyber Storm II were similar to challenges identified during the first Cyber Storm exercise. For example, comments regarding the need for better understanding of roles and responsibilities after Cyber Storm II were similar to comments made in four of the eight lessons resulting from Cyber Storm I. Also, both exercises resulted in comments calling for improvements to the exercise program and for better internal and external communications.

CONCLUSIONS

Both public and private sector participants in DHS's Cyber Storm exercises agreed that the exercises are valuable in helping them coordinate their responses to significant cyber incidents. After the completion of the first Cyber Storm exercise in February 2006, DHS identified 8 lessons and 66 activities to address these lessons, ranging from revising operating procedures to holding tabletop exercises to test and evaluate those revised procedures. While DHS has made progress in completing over 60 percent of these activities, it has more to do to complete key activities—including those that are planned for the future as well as those identified as ongoing without a completion date. More recently, key federal, state, and private sector officials who participated in the second Cyber Storm exercise in March 2008 observed areas of progress as well as continued challenges—many similar to challenges identified during the first exercise. Until DHS schedules and completes its corrective activities, the agency risks wasting resources on subsequent exercises that repeat the lessons it learned in 2006.

RECOMMENDATION FOR EXECUTIVE ACTION

Given the importance of continuously improving cyber exercises, we are making one recommendation to the Secretary of Homeland Security to direct the Assistant Secretary for Cybersecurity and Communications to ensure the scheduling and completion of the corrective actions addressing lessons learned during Cyber Storm I before conducting the next Cyber Storm Exercise.

AGENCY COMMENTS AND OUR EVALUATION

We received written comments on a draft of this chapter from DHS (see app. IV). In the department's response, the Director of the Departmental GAO/Office of Inspector General Liaison Office concurred with our recommendation and stated that DHS will continue to address actions related to Cyber Storm I findings. DHS also reported that after receiving the draft chapter, it has completed additional items, raising the percentage of corrective actions completed to over 70 percent. We did not modify the status of the activities identified in our chapter because DHS has not yet provided sufficient evidence to demonstrate that these activities have been completed.

In its comments, DHS also stated that end dates are not applicable for many of the remaining corrective actions because they are either dependent upon outside stakeholder actions or are ongoing or long-term activities that are being addressed incrementally over time. However, we found that most of the remaining activities are finite in nature and could be associated with a time frame. For example, it would be possible to establish time frames for issuing guidance to the information sharing and analysis centers on public communications, requesting that all computer emergency response teams have secure communications, and identifying international counterparts to NCRCG. Further, while we agree that some activities may involve other stakeholders or take more time, it is important for DHS to identify interim and final milestones for these activities so that they can monitor their progress. This approach is consistent with DHS's guidance for its exercise programs, which requires that each corrective action have a time frame for implementation.

DHS officials also provided technical comments, which we have incorporated as appropriate.

David A. Powner
Director, Information Technology Management Issues

APPENDIX I: OBJECTIVES, SCOPE, AND METHODOLOGY

Our objectives were to (1) identify the lessons that the Department of Homeland Security (DHS) learned from the first Cyber Storm exercise, (2) assess DHS's efforts to implement lessons learned from this exercise, and (3) identify key participants' views of their experiences during the second Cyber Storm exercise.

To identify the lessons learned from DHS's cyber attack simulations, we reviewed the agency's Cyber Storm Exercise Report. We also interviewed agency officials to obtain clarification on this exercise and the lessons learned.

To assess DHS's efforts to address the lessons it learned from its exercise, we analyzed DHS's list of planned activities and the status of these activities. We analyzed documentation of the activities that were reported as completed, including concepts of operations and standard operating procedures for relevant organizations as well as evidence of additional staff hires and completion of tabletop exercises. We also visited the United States Computer Emergency Readiness Team (US-CERT) to observe network and technology changes that were made to address lessons identified during Cyber Storm I. We interviewed DHS officials from the National Cyber Security Division (NCSD) and US-CERT to obtain clarification on documentation and plans.

To identify key participants' views of their experiences during the second Cyber Storm exercise, we interviewed Cyber Storm planners, observers, and participants from federal agencies, state governments, and the private sector. Specifically, we interviewed representatives from the Departments of Transportation, Justice, and Energy because these organizations were identified by DHS as key participants in the Cyber Storm exercises—either as an organization that was subject to simulated cyber incidents or as an organization critical to the recovery from the incidents. We interviewed the Multi-State Information Sharing and Analysis Center (ISAC) because it was able to represent multiple state governments that participated in the exercises. We also interviewed private sector officials representing the Information Technology ISAC, the Electricity ISAC, and the chemical sector. We asked participants about the issues raised during Cyber Storm I and whether these were improved or remained as challenges during Cyber Storm II. After discussing both Cyber Storm exercises with these participants, we analyzed their observations for commonalities and organized them into broad categories. These observations are not intended to be generalized to other exercise participants.

We performed our work at the headquarters of the Departments of Homeland Security, Transportation, Energy, and Justice and in Washington, D.C. In addition, we attended the Cyber Storm II exercise held in Washington, D.C., in March 2008.

We performed our work from January 2008 to September 2008 in accordance with generally accepted government auditing standards. Those standards require that we plan and perform the audit to obtain sufficient, appropriate evidence to provide a reasonable basis for our findings and conclusions based on our audit objectives. We believe that the evidence obtained provides a reasonable basis for our findings and conclusions based on our audit objectives.

APPENDIX II: DHS ACTIVITIES TO ADDRESS LESSONS FROM CYBER STORM I

DHS identified 66 activities to address lessons identified in Cyber Storm I. Almost half of these activities are intended to address multiple lessons. Table 4 shows the list of activities and which lessons they are intended to address.

Table 4. DHS's Planned Activities and the Lessons They Address

Activity identification number	DHS activity	Lesson(s) targeted by this activity[a]
1.	Significantly revise standard operating procedures for the National Cyber Response Coordination Group (NCRCG)	1, 2, 3, 4, 5, 7, 8
2.	Refine definition of Cyber Incident of National Significance	1
3.	Conduct meeting with member agencies to ensure they understand the needed resources to support NCRCG during activation	1
4.	Establish in standard operating procedures a means of quickly and clearly communicating changes in NCRCG engagement status with interfacing organizations	1, 4
5.	Within standard operating procedures, refine situation reports and situation report development and communication procedures	1, 4, 5, 7, 8
6.	Research and procure appropriate situation awareness visualization and communication tools	1
Activity identification number	DHS activity	Lesson(s) targeted by this activity[a]
7.	Request access to classified DHS networks in NCRCG's room	1, 4, 5, 7, 8
8.	Hold meeting among NCRCG, Homeland Security Operations Center, Interagency Advisory Council (now the Crisis Action Team), and US-	1

	CERT	
9.	Conduct a tabletop exercise among NCRCG, the Homeland Security Operations Center, the Interagency Advisory Council (now the Crisis Action Team), and US-CERT	1
10.	Work with the Office of Public Affairs to ensure NCRCG receives situation reports	1
11.	Provide a liaison to an interfacing group from NCRCG	1
12.	During the meeting in June 2006 with international participants, discuss coordination with entities similar to NCRCG	1
13.	Clarify interfaces and expectation at every level of NCRCG engagement	1, 7
14.	Move triage capability into US-CERT main facility	1, 3, 5
15.	Create four new positions to ensure staffing and continuity in US-CERT through normal and emergency operations	1, 7
16.	Refine and prioritize use and purposes of key US-CERT communications portals to eliminate redundancy and streamline communication with subscribers and counterparts	1, 4
17.	Meet in June 2006 with all international participants to share capabilities and establish working relationships	1, 2, 3, 4
18.	Discuss an initial international participant tabletop exercise and additional follow-on exercise activities with international participants and policy representatives in order to build clear way ahead for Cyber Storm II in 2008	1, 3
19.	Coordinate support of DHS's Operations office as noted in its revised standard operation procedures	1, 3, 4, 5, 7
20.	Once refined standard operating procedures are established for NCRCG, US-CERT, National Operations Center, and Interagency Advisory Council (now the Crisis Action Team) organize and support the tabletop exercise to validate and refine interaction	1
21.	Support the development of a contact list of key public and private sector subject matter experts	1, 4, 5

Table 4. (Continued).

Activity identification number	DHS activity	Lesson(s) targeted by this activitya
22.	Once clear engagement thresholds are established, ensure that all interfacing organizations are aware of thresholds, levels of engagement, and implications of each	1
23.	Establish a mechanism for communicating real world implications of cyber incidents to DHS Public Affairs and the Public Affairs Working Group	1, 6
24.	Modify standard operating procedures to reflect any changes in Homeland Security Advisory System policy	1, 3
25.	Work to identify and contact NCRCG counterpart organizations within international partners	1, 2, 4
26.	Develop the capability to reach back to the private sector	1
27.	Move to develop public affairs messaging coordination among NCRCG, NCSD, the Information Technology Information Sharing and Analysis Center, and the Information Technology Sector Coordinating Council for both normal and emergency operations	1, 3, 6
28.	Engage in conversations with leadership to frame possible changes in rules for raising alert levels based on threats to cross-sector support structure	1, 3
29.	Establish processes, procedures, and physical means to communicate securely with NCRCG counterparts at a policy level	1, 2, 4
30.	Once Situation Awareness Toolset is established, arrange for appropriate centers to have it	1, 4
31.	In meeting with international participants, address coordination of standard operating procedures and concept of operations	1
32.	Work to establish secure communications with all international partners	1
33.	Procure Government Emergency Telecommunications Service cards for all NCRCG members	2
34.	Research secure cell phone capability for NCRCG members	2
35.	Work with a foreign computer emergency response team to cosponsor another foreign computer emergency response team into an intragovernmental incident response forum	2
36.	Install Critical Infrastructure Warning Information Network terminal in US-CERT	2

Activity identification number	DHS activity	Lesson(s) targeted by this activity[a]
37.	Add redundant network support to US-CERT	2
38.	Procure 15 satellite phones	2
39.	Work to identify and organize a private sector counterpart for NCRCG with appropriate concepts of operations and standard operating procedures	2, 4, 5, 7
40.	Address public policy issues for industry incident response activities in cooperation with the industry and leadership	2
41.	Facilitate the development and implementation of cyber risk assessment methodologies across the information technology sector and in coordination with other sectors	2
42.	Coordinate standard operating procedures and concepts of operations with several ISACs	2, 3, 5
43.	Submit request for continuity-of-operations space and establish continuity-of-operations Plan	2
44.	Research alternatives to the Emergency Notification System	3
45.	Add dedicated support staff person to focus on processes and procedures	3
46.	Establish better e-mail connection during exercise to avoid spam filtering of injects	3, 5
47.	Execute semiannual tabletop exercise with accompanying education workshops focused on high-risk scenarios and cyber risk assessment	3, 5, 7, 8
48.	Coordinate standard operating procedures with US-CERT and the Information Technology and Communication ISACs	3, 4
49.	Transfer ticket tracking system over to an industry standard relational database tracking system for better correlation, analysis, and communication of incidents	3, 8
50.	Fill open spots with qualified personnel to gain bandwidth necessary to better address all aspects of US-CERT mission	3, 8
51.	Continue to expand network of informal and semiformal relationships with cyber-related associations and interest groups	4
52.	Forward request to require all federal computer emergency response teams to have secure communications, up to at least Secret	4, 7
53.	Request additional NCRCG support staff to address planning, correlation, and communication requirements	5

Table 4. (Continued).

Activity identification number	DHS activity	Lesson(s) targeted by this activity[a]
54.	Plan for significant pre-Cyber Storm II intelligence and law enforcement buildup exercise segment	5
55.	Complete permanent home of US-CERT, allowing classified operations to occur on-site	5
56.	Work to educate law enforcement on role and function of the NCRCG and establish sharing of cyber issues	5, 7
57.	Work to expedite tear-line policies (policies for organizing official documents so that unclassified information can be easily separated from classified information and disseminated)	5, 7
58.	Advocate inclusion of cyber public affairs in all exercises where appropriate	6
59.	Issue guidance to ISACs on a set of policies for cybersecurity-related public communications	6
60.	Establish baseline of public messaging based on cyber probable scenarios to include best channels for message delivery	6
61.	Develop comprehensive set of cyber scenarios to support exercises and planning	7
62.	Develop reporting process in coordination with reporting entities	8
63.	Participate in Internet Disruption Working Group tabletop exercise	8
64.	Plan and support cyber aspects of Top Officials 4 exercise	8
65.	Plan and execute Cyber Storm II	8
66.	Coordinate and develop situation report reporting process with National Operations Center and NCRCG	8

Source: GAO analysis of DHS data.

[a] The lessons are

Lesson 1: Interagency Coordination Groups
Lesson 2: Contingency Planning, Risk Assessment, and Roles and Responsibilities
Lesson 3: Integration of Incidents across Infrastructures
Lesson 4: Access to Information
Lesson 5: Coordination of Response Activities
Lesson 6: Strategic Communications and Public Relations
Lesson 7: Processes, Tools, and Technology
Lesson 8: The Exercise Program

APPENDIX III: GAO ANALYSIS OF DHS EFFORTS TO ADDRESS LESSONS FROM CYBER STORM I

Lessons	Activities 1	2	3	4	5	6	7	8	9	10	11	12	13	14	15	16	17	18	19	20	21	22	23	24	25	26	27	28	29	30	31	32	33
Lesson 1: Interagency Coordination Groups	+	+	+	+	+	+	+	+	+	+	+	+	+	+	+	+	+	+	+	+	+	+	+	0	0	0	0	0	0	>	+	>	
Lesson 2: Contingency Planning, Risk Assessment, and Roles and Responsibilities	+																+								0				0				+
Lesson 3: Integration of Incidents across Infrastructures	+													+			+	+	+					0			0	0					
Lesson 4: Access to Information	+			+	+		+									+	+		+		+				0				0	>			
Lesson 5: Coordination of Response Activities	+				+		+							+					+		+												
Lesson 6: Strategic Communications and Public Relations Plan																							+				0						
Lesson 7: Processes, Tools, and Technology	+				+		+						+		+				+														
Lesson 8: The Exercise Program	+				+		+																										

Lessons	Activities 34	35	36	37	38	39	40	41	42	43	44	45	46	47	48	49	50	51	52	53	54	55	56	57	58	59	60	61	62	63	64	65	66
Lesson 1: Interagency Coordination Groups																																	
Lesson 2: Contingency Planning, Risk Assessment, and Roles and Responsibilities	+	+	+	+	+	0	0	0	>	>																							
Lesson 3: Integration of Incidents across Infrastructures									>		+	+	+	+	>	>	>																
Lesson 4: Access to Information						0									>			0	0														
Lesson 5: Coordination of Response Activities						0			>				+	+						±	+	+	0	0									
Lesson 6: Strategic Communications and Public Relations Plan																									0	0	0						
Lesson 7: Processes, Tools, and Technology						0								+					0				0	0				+					
Lesson 8: The Exercise Program														+		>	>												+	+	+	+	+

Key:
+ - Completed and validated
± - Completed but not validated
0 - Ongoing
> - Planned for the future
A blank box indicates the activity is not applicable to the lesson

Source: GAO analysis of DHS data.

Figure 1. Activity Status, as of June 2008, by Lesson.

Figure 1 shows, for each lesson learned during Cyber Storm I, the status of the activity as reported by DHS and whether the status could be validated by GAO. The activities are identified by number in appendix II.

APPENDIX IV: COMMENTS FROM THE DEPARTMENT OF HOMELAND SECURITY

U.S. Department of Homeland Security
Washington, DC 20528

August 22, 2008

Mr. David Powner
Director
Information Technology Management Issues
United States Government Accountability Office
441 G Street, N.W.
Washington, DC 20548

Dear Mr. Powner:

Thank you for the opportunity to review and comment on the Government Accountability Office's (GAO's) draft report entitled CRITICAL INFRASTRUCTURE PROTECTION: DHS Needs to Fully Address Lessons Learned from Its First Cyber Storm Exercise (GAO-08-825). Technical comments have been provided under separate cover.

The Department of Homeland Security's (DHS's) efforts to develop and refine procedures for addressing and tracking corrective actions have benefited from this GAO engagement. DHS fully agrees with GAO assertions that continuous progress and validation of exercise findings is essential to improving our Nation's cyber security, preparedness posture, and ensuring the best use of resources.

GAO states in its draft report that DHS addressed and completed 43 of the 66 corrective actions. The remaining 23 corrective actions included 16 items labeled "ongoing" and 7 items labeled "planned for the future." DHS addressed and completed over 66 percent of the total corrective actions at the time the GAO's report was drafted. Since the release of GAO's draft report, DHS completed additional items, raising the percentage of corrective actions completed to over 70 percent. A full breakdown of recent actions undertaken and discussion of their status is enclosed as Appendix A.

Recommendation: *Given the importance of continuously improving cyber exercises, we are making one recommendation to the Secretary of Homeland Security to direct the Assistant Secretary for Cybersecurity and Communications to ensure the scheduling and completion of the corrective actions addressing lessons learned during Cyber Storm I before conducting the next Cyber Storm exercise.*

Response: DHS concurs with the draft GAO report's recommendation and will continue to address actions related to Cyber Storm I findings. Many of the remaining corrective actions, however, are inherently long-term or ongoing in nature. Some corrective actions are within DHS's direct power to manage or perform, while others require extensive coordination with stakeholders.

Fulfilling the report's recommendation that the Department take action to ensure these remaining corrective actions are scheduled and completed before executing the next Cyber Storm exercise is dependent on various factors. DHS suggests that the remaining corrective actions are either: (1) *long-term* activities and are being incrementally addressed over time; (2) dependent upon *outside*

www.dhs.gov

stakeholder action; or (3) *ongoing*, addressed in different capacities over time, and a specific "end date" does not apply.

DHS appreciates the thorough analysis and very constructive points raised by the GAO draft report. To best capitalize on this analysis and recommendation, DHS plans an enhanced emphasis on how corrective action categories are defined for purposes of planning and integration into future exercises. DHS is willing to work with GAO as these efforts go forward. Finally, we ask that GAO modify the report to reflect the additional items the National Cyber Security Division (NCSD) has completed since the draft report's release.

Thank you again for the opportunity to comment on this draft report and we look forward to working with you on future homeland security issues.

Sincerely,

Jerald E. Levine
Director
Departmental GAO/OIG Liaison Office

Enclosure

REFERENCES

[1] The White House, *National Strategy to Secure Cyberspace* (Washington, D.C.: February 2003), and Homeland Security Presidential Directive 7: Critical Infrastructure Identification, Prioritization, and Protection (Dec. 17, 2003).

[2] GAO, Critical Infrastructure Protection: Department of Homeland Security Faces *Challenges in Fulfilling Cybersecurity Responsibilities*, GAO-05-434 (Washington, D.C.: May 26, 2005); *Critical Infrastructure Protection: Challenges in Addressing Cybersecurity*, GAO-05-827T (Washington, D.C.: July 19, 2005); *Internet Infrastructure: DHS Faces Challenges in Developing a Joint Public/Private Recovery Plan*, GAO-06-672 (Washington, D.C.: June 16, 2006); *Internet Infrastructure: Challenges in Developing a Public/Private Recovery Plan*, GAO-06-863T (Washington, D.C.: July 28, 2006); *Critical Infrastructure Protection: DHS Leadership Needed to Enhance Cybersecurity Elements*, GAO-06-1087T (Washington, D.C.: Sept. 13, 2006); *Critical Infrastructure Protection: Multiple Efforts to*

Secure Control Systems Are Under Way, but Challenges Remain, GAO-07-1036 (Washington, D.C.: Sept. 10, 2007); *Critical Infrastructure Protection: Multiple Efforts to Secure Control Systems Are Under Way, but Challenges Remain*, GAO-08-119T (Washington, D.C.: Oct. 17, 2007); *Critical Infrastructure Protection: Sector- Specific Plans' Coverage of Key Cyber Security Elements Varies*, GAO-08-113 (Washington, D.C.: Oct. 31, 2007).

[3] DHS reported that one other activity had been completed, but the department was unable to provide evidence demonstrating its completion.

[4] The law and policies include the Homeland Security Act of 2002 (Pub. L. No. 107-296, Nov. 25, 2002); Homeland Security Presidential Directive 7: Critical Infrastructure Identification, Prioritization, and Protection (Dec. 17, 2003); and *The National Strategy to Secure Cyberspace* (February 2003).

[5] GAO, Cyber Analysis and Warning: DHS Faces Challenges in Establishing a Comprehensive National Capability, GAO-08-588 (Washington, D.C.: July 31, 2008).

[6] The Department of Justice's Computer Crime and Intellectual Property Section and the Department of Defense also cochair this group.

[7] Homeland Security Presidential Directive 8: National Preparedness (Dec. 17, 2003) and *The National Strategy to Secure Cyberspace* (February 2003).

[8] Department of Homeland Security, *National Infrastructure Protection Plan* (Washington, D.C.: June 2006).

[9] The Interagency Incident Management Group was later reorganized and renamed the Crisis Action Team.

[10] Homeland Security Presidential Directive 8: National Preparedness (Dec. 17, 2003).

[11] Department of Homeland Security, *Homeland Security Exercise and Evaluation Program* (Washington, D.C.: 2007).

INDEX

A

academic, 57, 83
access, 7, 8, 9, 17, 19, 26, 37, 77, 88, 93, 100
accessibility, 63
accidents, 80
accuracy, 24, 33
activation, 95, 100
administrators, 23, 60
age, 63
agents, 83
agriculture, 57, 72, 81
air, 64
air traffic, 64
alternative, 22, 32
alternatives, 32, 93, 103
analysts, 17, 20, 21, 30, 32, 39, 40, 42, 44, 45, 60
anomalous, 3, 18, 19, 21, 26, 29, 30, 42, 71
antivirus software, 20
appendix, 64, 65, 77, 92, 106
application, 34
assessment, 25, 70, 93
assets, 3, 4, 16, 18, 19, 21, 24, 28, 57, 65, 68, 70, 71, 72, 78, 81, 82, 83
attacker, 22, 25
attacks, vii, 2, 3, 4, 6, 7, 8, 10, 11, 12, 13, 16, 17, 18, 19, 20, 22, 23, 26, 30, 35, 38, 39, 41, 42, 45, 60, 61, 64, 65, 67, 70, 71, 76, 78, 81, 82, 83, 85, 87, 88, 89, 90
auditing, 3, 49, 62, 77, 100
Australia, 34
authority, 5, 12, 36, 37, 43, 44, 45, 46, 67
automation, 59
automobiles, 79
aviation, 81
awareness, 15, 20, 26, 27, 28, 29, 34, 35, 44, 82, 83, 87, 88, 89, 91, 92, 100

B

bandwidth, 103
banking, 57, 72, 76, 86
banks, 9, 10, 79
behavior, 15, 30
benefits, 2, 6, 38, 63, 76
breakdown, 96
buildings, 80
buses, 81

C

call centers, 9
Canada, 34
candidates, 42, 43
capacity, 12, 44
cell, 9, 93, 102
cell phones, 9

Central Intelligence Agency, 7, 8
centralized, 13, 43, 64
certification, 71
channels, 104
chemical industry, 79
chemicals, 83
Chernobyl, 8
China, 10, 58
citizens, 7
civilian, 20, 28
clinics, 81
coalitions, 83
collaboration, 15, 21, 35, 70, 88
commercial bank, 79
Committee on Homeland Security, 2, 76
Committee on Intelligence, 57
communication, 3, 16, 17, 34, 87, 88, 90, 92, 93, 94, 96, 97, 100, 101, 103
communities, 32
community, 6, 7, 15, 29, 48, 59, 71, 78, 89, 90, 91, 93, 95
competitor, 42
compilation, 28
complement, 5, 36, 66
complexity, 41
compliance, 59
components, 33, 80, 81
computer systems, 6, 35, 76
computer use, 35
computer virus, 8, 9, 11
confidence, 8, 90
confusion, 46, 90, 95
Congress, 58
connectivity, 2
constraints, 27
construction, 79
content analysis, 27, 44
contingency, 69, 77, 88, 89, 93, 94
continuity, 70, 93, 101, 103
contractors, 7, 10
contracts, 28
control, 6, 10, 24, 62, 63, 64, 65, 68, 69
corporations, 86
correlation, 19, 94, 103
correlations, 16

coverage, 59
credibility, 39
credit, 9
crime, 7
criminals, 6, 8, 9, 61, 64
crisis management, 70
critical assets, 4, 19, 24, 68
critical infrastructure, 6, 8, 10, 11, 12, 14, 17, 20, 25, 26, 28, 29, 30, 40, 41, 43, 44, 47, 57, 59, 61, 62, 63, 66, 67, 68, 69, 70, 72, 76, 77, 78, 79, 80, 82, 84, 85, 88
crop production, 79
customers, 4, 27, 30, 33, 36, 39, 40, 44
cybercrime, 64
cybersecurity, 5, 11, 12, 13, 14, 15, 27, 30, 31, 37, 39, 41, 42, 43, 46, 49, 61, 62, 63, 64, 65, 67, 68, 69, 70, 71, 76, 77, 79, 81, 82, 87, 92, 94, 104
cyberspace, 12, 70, 71, 76, 79, 82

D

data collection, 59
data set, 42
database, 59, 94, 103
decision makers, 96
decision making, 83, 87
decisions, 16, 17, 25
defense, 10, 57, 72
definition, 89, 100
Delaware, 84, 85
delivery, 11, 20, 104
denial, 7, 8, 10, 64
Department of Agriculture, 79, 81
Department of Defense (DOD), 1, 6, 10, 47, 80, 108
Department of Energy, 29, 33, 48, 80
Department of Health and Human Services, 79, 81
Department of Homeland Security, vii, 1, 2, 11, 14, 48, 49, 58, 61, 73, 75, 76, 79, 80, 81, 99, 106, 107, 108
Department of Justice, 13, 37, 108
Department of the Interior, 81
destruction, 10, 57, 72, 78

detection, 19, 20, 21, 26, 27, 44, 46, 59
deterrence, 11, 71
Director of National Intelligence, 57
disabled, 78
disaster, 84
discipline, 41
disclosure, 41
disseminate, 14, 33, 90, 91
distribution, 33, 64, 80
download, 7, 35
draft, 5, 46, 78, 98

E

earthquake, 84
economic losses, 78
economic security, 10, 57, 72, 78
egg, 81
electric power, 64, 78, 80
electricity, 59, 80, 83
emergency medical services, 80
emergency response, 20, 94, 98, 102, 103
employees, 6, 7, 10, 12
employment, 9
energy, 57, 72, 76, 84, 86
engagement, 94, 100, 101, 102
environment, 8, 16, 17, 18, 22, 32
environmental conditions, 18
Environmental Protection Agency, 80
espionage, 7
Estonia, 10, 37, 58, 64, 72
examinations, 22
execution, 91
exercise, 36, 60, 63, 67, 76, 77, 78, 82, 83, 84, 85, 86, 87, 88, 89, 90, 91, 92, 94, 95, 96, 97, 98, 99, 101, 103, 104
expert, 24, 66
expertise, 7, 12, 13, 16, 17, 21, 37, 42, 58, 82, 83
explosives, 83

F

failure, 89

false positive, 20, 21
fear, 42
Federal Bureau of Investigation, 6, 8, 37
federal government, 11, 13, 23, 26, 27, 43, 63, 67, 68, 76, 80, 82
federal law, 11, 64
feedback, 33
finance, 57, 72, 79, 86
financial institution, 9, 10, 76, 79, 85
financial institutions, 9, 10, 76, 79, 85
financial sector, 64, 86
fire, 80
flow, 3, 4, 5, 15, 18, 28, 30, 31, 42, 71, 90
focusing, 95
food, 57, 72, 79, 81
Food and Drug Administration, 79, 81
For Official Use Only, 33
foreign nation, 6
forensic, 22
fraud, 7, 9, 63
funds, 8, 79
fusion, 30, 43

G

GAO, 1, 4, 8, 9, 14, 15, 16, 18, 19, 30, 32, 33, 46, 47, 49, 58, 60, 61, 62, 65, 71, 72, 73, 75, 81, 86, 98, 104, 105, 106, 107, 108
gas, 80
Georgia, 49
goals, 71
government, 2, 3, 6, 9, 10, 11, 13, 14, 20, 23, 26, 27, 28, 29, 30, 34, 37, 41, 42, 43, 49, 57, 58, 59, 60, 62, 63, 64, 67, 68, 70, 71, 72, 76, 77, 78, 79, 80, 81, 82, 83, 84, 85, 86, 88, 90, 91, 97, 99, 100
groups, 4, 7, 8, 33, 36, 61, 64, 65, 67, 69, 77, 88, 92, 103
growth, 6, 76
guidance, 11, 13, 23, 25, 66, 68, 77, 91, 92, 94, 98, 104
Gulf Coast, 83

H

hackers, 6, 7, 10
handling, 14, 17, 18, 21, 23, 25, 43, 45, 60, 78, 93, 94, 95, 96
hands, 20
health, 15, 16, 22, 30, 57, 72, 79, 81
Health and Human Services, 79, 81
health care, 57, 72, 81
hearing, 61, 62
high risk, 72
high-risk, 41, 61, 103
highways, 81
hiring, 5, 12, 42, 44, 45, 46
homeland security, 41, 91
Homeland Security, vii, 1, 2, 5, 11, 12, 13, 14, 26, 34, 37, 43, 44, 45, 48, 49, 50, 58, 61, 71, 73, 75, 76, 78, 79, 80, 81, 82, 92, 97, 99, 100, 101, 102, 106, 107, 108
Homeland Security Act, 11, 58, 71, 108
hospitals, 81
host, 59
House, 2, 76
human, 9, 17, 27
hurricane, 83

I

id, 62, 66, 96
identification, 12, 32, 40, 100, 102, 103, 104
identity, 7, 9
Illinois, 85
implementation, 31, 46, 62, 81, 91, 98, 103
incentives, 68
incidents, 6, 10, 89, 104
inclusion, 104
Indiana, 49
indicators, 12, 20, 41, 45
industrial, 7, 57, 72, 80
industry, 6, 9, 24, 39, 67, 69, 71, 76, 77, 79, 83, 84, 85, 86, 87, 91, 94, 103
information exchange, 29
information sharing, 1, 4, 12, 14, 15, 20, 36, 41, 44, 47, 63, 64, 68, 69, 70, 76, 77, 79, 82, 87, 88, 92, 93, 94, 98
information system, 47
information systems, 12, 26, 28, 44, 70, 86, 96
information technology, 6, 34, 47, 48, 57, 59, 61, 70, 72, 80, 84, 85, 86, 87, 93, 94, 98, 99, 102, 103
infrastructure, 6, 8, 10, 11, 12, 13, 14, 17, 20, 24, 25, 26, 28, 29, 30, 34, 35, 40, 41, 42, 43, 44, 45, 47, 57, 59, 61, 62, 63, 65, 66, 68, 69, 70, 71, 72, 76, 77, 78, 79, 82, 83, 84, 85, 86, 87, 88, 94, 95, 96
insight, 15, 30
Inspector General, 98
instability, 43
institutions, 10, 57, 81, 83
insurance, 79
insurance companies, 79
integration, 66, 77, 88, 89, 93
integrity, 8, 59
intelligence, 6, 7, 8, 11, 15, 16, 17, 20, 29, 30, 32, 39, 48, 64, 104
interaction, 14, 49, 87, 88, 101
interest groups, 103
interface, 87
Internet, 6, 7, 8, 9, 13, 15, 16, 22, 24, 26, 28, 29, 30, 31, 35, 44, 48, 58, 59, 62, 64, 65, 69, 70, 73, 76, 82, 104, 107
interview, 47
interviews, 47, 48
intrusions, 7, 12, 20, 31
investigative, 21, 59, 96
ISC, 59

L

labor, 10
laptop, 9
large-scale, 7, 76, 83, 84, 86, 87
law, 2, 11, 15, 20, 21, 24, 29, 30, 32, 39, 41, 43, 64, 71, 78, 79, 80, 86, 93, 95, 104, 108
law enforcement, 11, 15, 20, 21, 24, 29, 30, 32, 39, 41, 43, 71, 78, 80, 86, 93, 95, 104
laws, 2, 11, 47, 59

lead, 11, 15, 22, 26, 35, 36, 46, 68, 79, 82, 89
leadership, 5, 36, 43, 87, 93, 102, 103
limitation, 28
limitations, 32, 36
local government, 11, 13, 20, 28, 30, 34, 37, 41, 57, 58, 64, 70, 71, 76, 79, 83, 86
logging, 10
long-term, 12, 43, 98
Los Angeles, 10

M

machinery, 81
maintenance, 6, 80
malicious, 8, 10, 19, 31, 42, 61, 63, 64
malware, 6, 7, 8, 22, 29, 31, 32, 37, 38
management, 5, 25, 46, 47, 59, 70, 82
manufacturing, 57, 72, 81
markets, 7
Maryland, 60
Massachusetts, 86
measurement, 59
measures, 12, 25, 33, 36, 38, 44, 90
meat, 81
media, 6, 20, 37, 38, 39, 90, 96
membership, 13, 37, 96
memory, 9
messages, 8, 9, 23, 88, 96
metropolitan area, 49
Microsoft, 48
military, 7, 20, 28, 80
missions, 68
mobility, 81
morale, 8
movement, 81
multidisciplinary, 17
mutual funds, 79

N

nation, vii, 2, 4, 6, 8, 10, 11, 13, 14, 26, 28, 30, 32, 38, 39, 40, 44, 45, 61, 62, 64, 65, 69, 71, 76, 78, 79, 80, 82, 88
nation states, 6, 38

national, vii, 2, 4, 5, 6, 8, 10, 11, 12, 13, 14, 15, 26, 28, 33, 36, 37, 41, 43, 44, 45, 47, 48, 49, 57, 60, 62, 64, 66, 70, 71, 72, 78, 79, 81, 82, 84, 85, 86, 87, 91, 95
National Institute of Standards and Technology (NIST), 1, 23, 25, 48, 59, 60
National Protection and Programs Directorate, 26, 30
National Science Foundation, 43
national security, 8, 57, 64, 71, 72, 78, 79, 87, 91
National Strategy, 11, 58, 71, 81, 107, 108
National Strategy to Secure Cyberspace, 11, 58, 71, 81, 107, 108
natural, 79, 80
natural gas, 80
Navy, 47
network, 2, 3, 4, 6, 7, 9, 14, 16, 18, 19, 20, 21, 22, 23, 24, 25, 26, 28, 29, 30, 31, 32, 35, 37, 40, 41, 43, 60, 62, 64, 65, 66, 71, 82, 86, 99, 103
New York, 84
New Zealand, 34
newspapers, 20
Norfolk, 49
normal, 3, 16, 18, 28, 71, 94, 101, 102
nuclear, 57, 72, 80
nuclear material, 80
nuclear reactor, 57, 72, 80

O

observations, 15, 48, 78, 95, 99
Office of Management and Budget (OMB), 1, 26
oil, 80
online, 7, 9
organization, 4, 5, 6, 7, 14, 17, 19, 24, 27, 28, 29, 30, 31, 32, 33, 36, 37, 38, 39, 40, 41, 43, 48, 59, 65, 67, 82, 85, 89, 95, 96, 99
organizations, 5, 7, 8, 10, 15, 17, 18, 19, 20, 23, 24, 25, 28, 33, 37, 38, 39, 42, 46, 47, 59, 60, 63, 64, 68, 71, 78, 80, 83, 87, 88, 89, 90, 91, 94, 95, 96, 97, 99, 100, 102
organized crime, 7

P

Pacific, 83, 84
packets, 19
pandemic, 84
paper, 34
partnerships, 12, 70, 76
Patent and Trademark Office, 58
Pennsylvania, 10, 49
pension, 79
performance, 3, 12, 21, 33, 36, 38, 44, 49, 68
perseverance, 41
personal, 9, 20, 41, 80
personal relations, 41
personal relationship, 41
pharmaceuticals, 79
phone, 93, 102
pipelines, 81
planning, 43, 62, 66, 69, 70, 76, 77, 86, 88, 89, 93, 94, 95, 103, 104
plants, 78
policymakers, 12
population, 7
posture, 37
poultry, 81
power, 7, 64, 78, 80, 81
preparedness, 13, 71, 83, 86
prevention, 11, 14, 19, 71
preventive, 90
priorities, 11, 22, 32
privacy, 23
private, 11, 13, 14, 23, 28, 29, 30, 31, 37, 39, 41, 42, 43, 57, 58, 59, 60, 62, 63, 64, 66, 67, 68, 69, 70, 71, 76, 77, 79, 81, 82, 83, 84, 85, 86, 87, 88, 89, 90, 91, 93, 94, 95, 96, 97, 99, 101, 102, 103
private sector, 11, 13, 23, 28, 29, 30, 31, 37, 39, 41, 42, 57, 58, 59, 60, 63, 66, 67, 68, 70, 71, 76, 79, 86, 87, 88, 89, 90, 93, 95, 96, 97, 99, 101, 102, 103
private-sector, 64
probability, 66
production, 76
productivity, 79
program, 3, 9, 15, 26, 27, 35, 42, 48, 67, 76, 77, 82, 88, 91, 94, 97
promote, 59, 71, 87
property, 80
protection, 11, 12, 14, 16, 19, 24, 40, 43, 47, 59, 61, 77, 79
protocols, 7, 15
public, 8, 9, 10, 11, 13, 14, 15, 22, 23, 24, 31, 34, 35, 41, 43, 57, 62, 63, 64, 67, 68, 69, 70, 71, 72, 76, 77, 78, 79, 80, 82, 86, 87, 88, 89, 90, 92, 93, 94, 95, 96, 97, 98, 101, 102, 103, 104
public affairs, 88, 90, 94, 96, 102, 104
public health, 10, 57, 72, 78, 79
public policy, 103
public relations, 77, 78, 88, 90, 94, 95, 96
pumping, 80

R

radiological, 85
rail, 81
range, 13, 44, 83, 91
raw material, 79
raw materials, 79
reaction time, 42
real time, 31, 42
recognition, 21
recovery, 11, 12, 13, 14, 25, 36, 44, 45, 62, 64, 69, 70, 76, 79, 81, 82, 86, 87, 99
recreational, 80
reduction, 12, 26, 35, 71, 76, 79
redundancy, 101
refining, 33, 77, 80, 91, 93
regional, 83, 84, 85
regulators, 41
relational database, 94, 103
relationships, 4, 5, 18, 20, 24, 36, 37, 41, 43, 44, 45, 46, 63, 68, 71, 87, 88, 89, 91, 93, 101, 103
relevance, 16, 21
reliability, 39
research, 3, 15, 17, 21, 48, 58, 59, 71, 80
research and development, 58, 71
reservoirs, 80

Index

resources, 4, 11, 18, 19, 22, 23, 24, 27, 32, 36, 65, 70, 94, 97, 100
responsibilities, 5, 11, 12, 14, 15, 39, 40, 46, 61, 62, 64, 65, 69, 70, 71, 76, 77, 78, 83, 88, 89, 90, 93, 95, 97
retail, 79
risk, 12, 19, 21, 24, 28, 32, 41, 61, 66, 67, 68, 69, 72, 77, 81, 88, 89, 93, 103
risk assessment, 28, 68, 77, 88, 89, 93, 103
risks, 2, 3, 6, 11, 17, 18, 19, 21, 22, 25, 28, 30, 61, 71, 76, 78, 89, 94, 97

S

sabotage, 9, 63
SAC, 99
safety, 10, 57, 72, 78, 79
sales, 79
SAR, 35
satellite, 81, 93, 103
scheduling, 97
scholarships, 27
scores, 59
scripts, 7
search, 9
Secret Service, 37
Secretary of Defense, 58
Secretary of Homeland Security, 5, 12, 26, 37, 44, 45, 78, 82, 97
sector-specific plans, 65
secure communication, 92, 94, 97, 98, 102, 103
security, 6, 8, 9, 10, 17, 19, 20, 24, 25, 28, 29, 30, 34, 39, 41, 47, 57, 58, 59, 60, 61, 63, 64, 68, 70, 71, 72, 76, 78, 79, 81, 82, 87, 91, 96
Senate, 57
sensitivity, 23, 33
series, 83
service provider, 31
services, 7, 8, 20, 21, 48, 57, 59, 72, 80, 81, 84
severity, 22, 25
shares, 30

sharing, 1, 4, 12, 14, 15, 20, 26, 29, 34, 35, 36, 40, 41, 44, 47, 48, 59, 63, 64, 68, 69, 70, 76, 77, 79, 82, 87, 88, 91, 92, 93, 94, 95, 96, 97, 98, 104
shipping, 57, 72, 81
signals, 17
simulation, 76
simulations, 25, 67, 83, 99
sites, 7, 9, 10, 21, 24, 35, 64, 80
situation awareness, 92, 100
software, 6, 9, 10, 17, 19, 24, 32, 59, 71, 80
solutions, 21
spam, 7, 8, 103
spectrum, 59
speed, 63, 91
sports, 80
spyware, 7, 8
stability, 5, 12, 36, 43, 44
stabilize, 95
staffing, 46, 101
stages, 26, 27, 35
stakeholder, 98
stakeholders, 12, 40, 45, 46, 60, 68, 69, 70, 84, 85, 87, 98
standard operating procedures, 93, 99, 100, 101, 102, 103
standards, 3, 20, 49, 59, 62, 77, 94, 100
storage, 6, 80
strategic, 11, 12, 13, 32, 37, 40, 66, 77, 82, 87, 88
strategies, 2, 45, 46, 47, 70
students, 27
subscribers, 101
suffering, 37
supply, 7, 79, 80, 81
supply chain, 79, 81
support staff, 103
symbolic, 80
systems, vii, 6, 7, 8, 9, 10, 12, 18, 19, 20, 24, 25, 26, 28, 34, 44, 57, 61, 62, 63, 65, 68, 69, 70, 71, 72, 76, 78, 79, 80, 81, 86, 89, 96

T

talent, 7

tanks, 10
targets, 7, 10
task force, 66
technology, 5, 6, 9, 19, 47, 76, 77, 80, 88, 92, 94, 96, 99
telecommunications, 59, 70, 76, 83, 84, 86
television, 20
territorial, 85
terrorist, 83
terrorist acts, 11
terrorist attack, 11, 41, 71, 78, 82
terrorists, 8, 61, 64
testimony, 26, 62, 63, 68, 70
The Homeland Security Act, 11
theft, 7, 9
threat, 2, 3, 7, 9, 11, 12, 16, 17, 18, 19, 20, 21, 22, 23, 24, 25, 26, 29, 30, 31, 32, 39, 40, 41, 59, 60, 62, 64, 65, 70, 71, 82, 85
threats, vii, 2, 3, 4, 6, 8, 11, 12, 13, 14, 15, 16, 18, 19, 20, 22, 24, 25, 26, 29, 30, 31, 36, 38, 39, 40, 41, 42, 44, 45, 49, 60, 61, 62, 64, 65, 70, 71, 78, 82, 83, 88, 89, 96, 102
thresholds, 23, 87, 102
time commitment, 27
time frame, 98
timetable, 67
TIP, 35
tracking, 103
traffic, 3, 8, 10, 15, 16, 18, 19, 26, 28, 29, 30, 31, 42, 44, 64, 71
traffic flow, 30
training, 42, 71, 91
transactions, 79, 80
transfer, 59
transmission, 76, 80
transnational, 8
transparent, 5, 45, 46
transportation, 48, 57, 72, 80, 81, 84, 85, 86, 87
travel, 66
Treasury, 79
trend, 22
triage, 16, 101
triggers, 21
Trojan horse, 9, 19

trucks, 81
trustworthiness, 21
turnover, 5, 41
two-way, 41

U

U.S. economy, 8
unclassified, 34, 96, 104
United Kingdom, 34
United States, vii, 1, 2, 6, 7, 11, 30, 37, 47, 57, 62, 70, 71, 72, 75, 81, 99
United States Computer Emergency Readiness Team (US-CERT), vii, 1, 2, 4, 5, 11, 13, 14, 15, 23, 25, 26, 27, 28, 29, 30, 31, 32, 33, 34, 35, 36, 37, 38, 39, 40, 41, 42, 43, 44, 45, 46, 47, 48, 49, 62, 65, 66, 75, 82, 89, 90, 92, 93, 96, 99, 100, 101, 102, 103, 104
United States Postal Service, 81

V

values, 81
variance, 68
velocity, 42
victims, 9
virus, 6, 9, 10, 58
viruses, 6, 8, 9, 19
visualization, 92, 100
voice, 9, 62, 66, 69
vulnerability, 9, 11, 12, 20, 21, 24, 29, 40, 59, 63, 68, 70, 76, 79

W

warfare, 6, 7, 10
water, 10, 57, 72, 78, 79, 80
weapons, 80
welfare, 16, 22
well-being, 79
wells, 80
White House, 34, 58, 73, 107
wireless, 9, 81

Index

working groups, 36, 69
workload, 5, 45

worm, 6, 8, 9
worms, 8, 9, 19